I Love the Word Impossible

I Love the Word Impossible

ANN KIEMEL

TYNDALE
House Publishers, Inc.
Wheaton, Illinois

The author and the publisher gratefully acknowledge permission from the Gaither Music Company to quote, on pages 128 and 150, from the song "Something Beautiful," © Copyright 1971 by William J. Gaither.

Library of Congress Catalog Card Number 75-42908
ISBN 8423-1575-6, cloth; ISBN 8423-1574-8, paper.

Eighth printing, November 1977

Over 175,000 copies in print

to my father and mother
who have lived great lives
and raised me to believe God and i, together,
could make it through ANYTHING.

and to my boss and friend and spiritual mentor,
dean robert helfrich.
his heart is stretched so wide,
and he is so honest.

and with love to Hal and Susie Zigelbaum

contents

preface

i love the word impossible...

it's like joy after sorrow.
        people being friends after being enemies.
        rainbows after drenching rain.
        a wound healed.
        sunsets on quiet evenings after
                      hot, noisy days.
        paralyzed, injured limbs learning to grow
                  strong and useful again.
        forgiveness after wrong.
        truth after fog.
        new love-made babies.
        birds learning to fly and own the sky.
        bitterness turned to mellowness.
        fresh, genuine hope ... once abandoned.
        people finding each other at right moments,
                in unexpected, obscure places...
                for God-ordained reasons.

i love that word impossible because my God believes in
   adventure
         and extraordinary mountains, and He dares
to be alive in a world crawling with terrible
                                    situations.

He promises to be bigger than any impossibility
         because He is love...
      and love always finds a way through,
         in time.
love isn't scared.
it builds bridges instead of walls.
it never gives up.
it always hangs on.
it waits with stubborn, strong hope.
         sometimes even years.

love makes God alive in far more than human souls.
   like sun and clear sky and drooping branches
         and dark birds and color and design and music...
   and the sound of water on a shore.

IMPOSSIBLE means that i,
      an ordinary young woman,
can be something special and significant
      in an enormous, hurting world.
i can be love where i live,
      and that is Christ...

and He really does make ALL
                     the difference!

one:
i'm a woman now

sunday night

it's sunday night.

i flew in this afternoon, as i do most sundays,
from speaking somewhere in the country. a garment
bag over one arm and books under the other ... and the
feeling that at any moment something was going to
drop or i would get tangled in my coat and sprawl.

i am always one of the first off the plane.
i walk very fast.
my car is usually parked in the airport garage
across from the terminal.

when i unlock the door to my little apartment, there
is no one to greet me ...

> no strong man to wrap me in his arms,
> to laugh with me in love and belonging, shedding my
> sophistication.

no one to hear whether i felt encouraged or disappointed
about people's receptiveness to me and my dreams.
no child to scoop up and squeeze and call my own.

it's amusing. a lot of people think my world is
glamorous. airplanes and hotels and faraway cities.

there are many special things i love and cherish...
and there are long layovers in enormous airports
   and cold hotel rooms on winter nights
   and crowds to stumble through,
   down endlessly long corridors,
as i try to get to a gate to catch a plane, dash and still miss it.
   and people who scrutinize me with a frown when i bound in
   the door of the auditorium, and days when i am feeling so
tired and so unattractive
      and i still have to smile and cover my insecurities and
   weariness in front of several hundred ... instead of going
home and hiding.

it had been a successful convention, and i was seated on a
TWA jet in st. louis, returning home. yummmmmm.
just as we started to pull away from the gate, engines stopped,
and a stewardess said,
      "evacuate immediately. this is an emergency. leave
   everything in your seats."
and we did...
for five hours. we were kept in an area of the airport
while they thoroughly investigated a bomb threat.
i felt drained and exhausted from a lot of speaking, and
devastated that i couldn't be on my way home.

when we finally reboarded, i turned to the man next to me.
      "how are you feeling?"
      "lousy ... yep, really lousy."

"me, too. you know, i could smack whoever gave that
bomb threat. sir, i'm a Christian. Jesus really is Lord of
my life, but i'm just not a 'miss pollyanna' in an
experience like this. sir, you know what i really love
about Jesus? i think He knows just how we feel."
the man threw his head back and roared with laughter.
        "you're the first Christian i ever met who makes it
        sound real and exciting..."

another day i arrived in a sunny, warm southern city to speak. i
wondered, as i deboarded, who would be there to meet me.
usually, i never know the people, and *they* identify *me*. that
day, no one did.

it was exactly thirty minutes before i was to be at a certain
hotel to address a banquet. the flight was long, and i needed
to change and freshen up. i wandered around the terminal area
awhile, hoping someone would claim me. i saw an older couple
stare a lot in my direction. they seemed like possible
candidates ... very conservative in their appearance, and it
was a church conference. they walked back and forth as i
leaned against a counter. finally, i had the air lines page,
        "party meeting ann kiemel ... please come to
        united's information desk...."

this couple did ... only five feet away ... just watching me. i
smiled shyly, hoping they would respond. then i became
paranoid.
        "what is it they don't like about me? my dress is long.
it has sleeves, the neckline is high, and i'm not gaudied up in
jewelry. i've got sandals on, but..."

suddenly the man, with wrinkled frown, called out,
        "do you know ann kiemel?"
i spilled into smiles ... "it's me! i'm ann."

17

they didn't smile. nor offer to carry my bag. they walked ahead
of me in silence, and led me to their car parked at the far end of
the airport. they crawled in the front seat and closed their
doors, and i sheepishly got in back. nothing was said as we
drove to the hotel. the man again parked far from the entrance,
and neither helped me crawl out or offered to carry my things.
when we got inside, they pressed the elevator button for the
banquet room, and i became frantic...

      "sir, my room! i must change..."

he shrugged his shoulders, so i marched to the desk and
registered myself. and when i turned to go my eyes caught the
wife with another woman, shaking her head in negative
dismay.

when i got to my room, i fell across the bed and sobbed.
      "Jesus, i can't go down there to that banquet. they
      don't like me. i won't fit in. i'm going to be rejected
      without even being heard. i'm so scared..."

for a few minutes, i forgot time. i didn't care. i could only
wail. then i pulled myself up, washed my face, changed clothes
and walked out with a straight back, my head high, and my eyes
very red. someone there had faith enough to call me to do this,
and God would help me. i walked into the large banquet
room, and was instantly greeted by warm, charming people
with strong handshakes and wide smiles. i couldn't even find the
couple who picked me up...
      until afterward.

      after i had spoken, and God had powerfully graced the
      evening, then they decided i was "okay" ... the little
      wife grabbed me and led me through the crowd, telling
      everyone she and her husband had brought me from
      the airport. sighhhhh.

i have flown next to someone who poured a whole can of beer in her lap ... another who had an awful case of nausea which made me almost have one too.

people have whisked me into an enormous, cold auditorium on a stormy night, and i was genuinely at God's mercy to bring some warmth and beauty. in one city, it was over a hundred degrees outside, 800 people were packed into a high school auditorium where the air conditioning had failed, and babies screamed and 300 fans waved vigorously. i wondered if i could possibly communicate through all that ... and i can testify that God has been absolutely faithful. he's come through every time.

it makes me laugh now when i think of youth camps and summer retreats where i've been dropped off at the "workers' cabin" ... some workers' cabins have spiders on the walls and musty smells, and i'm not a very good "rougher." the lovely part is that it takes only a few hours until everyone belongs, and i feel so much a part, and rather than the awful loneliness at first, i begin to feel a kindred spirit, enriched and graced and mellowed by the earthy goodness of others. and i find myself going to sleep without being afraid of bugs.

probably women with homes and husbands and children forget those parts of traveling and being "public" ... and i forget that with husbands and children come meals to prepare and laundry to do and floors to keep scrubbed and noses wiped and lunches to pack. i think we are both lucky. God has a creative way of giving the romantic and awe-inspiring and bright without ignoring the humdrum and nitty-gritty and sobering.

one woman once wrote,
"no wonder you can speak with confidence and grace. you have the whole world on your side. you travel and eat out and meet people everywhere and are young. i cannot be a

happy Christian. i've been married and divorced three times, had
a nervous breakdown, and am trapped at home."
i responded by letter...
"your life sounds very difficult. i'm so sorry it's been so rough
for you. behind my sunshine and what you call 'grace' are some
enormous disappointments and shameful failures and lonely
agonies. i think no one escapes life without pain and
struggle. try and remember that it's how we let God help us
respond that determines whether or not we can live with hope. i
believe in bright happy tomorrows for you..."

new year's eve

it matters what you do with a year.
it counts. the old is the foundation
for the new.

new year's eve, 1974.
i threw a robe over my gown, slipped on sandals.
a warm cap over my ears, and gloves.
my world was black with night. the cold caught my
breath and made it white, and i laughed to
watch it and feel its sting on my face.
everything was still and quiet. i scraped up a
ball of snow and aimed it at the neighbors' window.
i threw three more and waited for them to look
out ... and laugh back ... and belong and BE at
the dawn of '75.

then i tossed snowballs in the night ... in all directions.
and called out,
"God, do you see me?
ann. in this old neighborhood. i'm alive, God.
i'm celebrating. YOU'VE made me live.

You've kept me strong. when i hurt, You did.
when i cried, You cried. when i failed, You knew ... but
You didn't shove me away. others would have.
they would have thought their judgment righteous and
proper. oh Jesus, not You.
    You're love.
    and love is strong. and faithful. and loyal.
    and patient and kind.
Jesus, thank you.
'74 had agony and promise.
i still want to know so much more about Truth.
but i'm growing. i can feel it, God.
make 'something beautiful' out of me.
    it's a NEW year. yahoooooo..."

snowballs and flurries and miles of sky and bending trees.
and God and i and love
    wanting to turn the world.
        in small ways.
            where people live and hurt.
because He loves us.
you. me.
anyone.

earlier that new year's eve, i popped corn in my new popper from
Christmas ... and took it downstairs to the girls who live below
me. We sipped Pepsis and stretched on the rug to watch t.v.
then they poured me eggnog, and we felt festive and
sophisticated, waiting for a new year.

today the unknown hours stretch and pull before me.
potential and power and poise.
eternity in my neighborhood, where i live ... i believe.

i'm a woman now

i'm ann, and i'm a woman now.
twenty-nine years old.
eight years out of college,
through three jobs.
with enough experiences to produce some maturity.

when i started speaking, i often defined myself as
"a simple, young girl." that is a secure feeling and i
find myself still tempted to use it.
i feel as if i must be twenty.
there's zest and energy and enthusiasm inside.
but no longer can people muse.
   "she is so young to have done so many things. she's just fresh
  in the real world. we must give her room to grow."
      it isn't that perfection is demanded.
    just some discretion, a balance in opinions.
      sensibleness.
      whatever i now achieve, with God's help,
       will no longer be phenomenal, but expected.
    being grown up can be scary. no more room
     for excuses.

as a child in a conservative evangelical home,
    truth was black and white;
    life, cut and dried.
by the time i reached college,
i was self-assured about my stability
and wisdom to control
    whatever rough spots came along.
there might be pain and struggle,
but God and i would come through.
i knew ann.
ann had foundation.
she was strong. now,
several years later, i'm amazed
at how poorly i sometimes came through
(certainly no blame on God),
and shocked at how confused i
    was in situations i always felt
convinced i could handle.

today, truth does not stare at me
    in black and white. at times
i find myself "seeking and searching with all my heart,"
and then taking a step and simply asking God
    to show me clearly if it is wrong.
i believe His love promises to do that.
a mind-boggling experience was discovering, suddenly,
that all Christians did not have the same interpretations
of Scripture or life. strong Christians!
        with deep faith
        and poised spirits that had been
            mellowed by all kinds of tragedy and years.
at a baptist convention i addressed, i casually
mentioned over dinner how much i loved the theology
of e. stanley jones. people
cleared their throats and coughed and mumbled out negatives.

a long-time devout Christian woman
told me she thought sins of passion were more forgivable than
breaking of the sabbath—even going out after church on
sunday nights for refreshments.
(lots of people in my church flock to restaurants on sunday
nights.)
admired Christian writers strongly disagree
with one another on various issues.
somehow, i grew up without realizing
that there is more than one way for married partners to be
unfaithful to each other. speaking to a denominational meeting
of my church, a man told me how he had been persecuted
for changing over from the other denomination, charged now
as a non-evangelical.

as a young woman, i must internalize for myself what i shall
live and die by.
i must open myself wide to God and decide
through all the varying feelings and opinions and
interpretations what is honestly right and real for me, what
will be true to my integrity.

no, life isn't so simple now.
it can be complex and sometimes very frightening.
in my traveling i have met many people ... Christians ... with
seemingly impossible situations. there are not a lot of easy
answers. sometimes i cannot even think of one. people call for
advice. i have no pat answers. i can share what is right for
me, what the Bible says about various things ... but i don't
know where people are coming from, or all the wounded parts of
their emotions.
i cannot make judgments.

       i don't believe Jesus Christ asks that from me. He
       wants me to listen. to give warmth and love. to try and
       help a person grasp God in his/her life and decide,

through God, what is truth for him or her. to
understand the power of total commitment.
but judgment, no.
i've not walked anyone else's road; i've not carried others'
crosses.
i've not felt their childhood. i've never crawled behind their
skin where hearts and minds beat.
only God has.
only i know me, and only God and i, alone, know what
place God has in my life ... and if what i say is honest.

often people talk of being afraid of God.
i'm not. people, yes. God, no.
God knows me through and through. He's fair. He's kind.
and forgiving and longsuffering. He places no stigmas, ever.

people ... that's something else. they (Christians as much as
any) can be impatient and critical and harsh. they are so
individualistic, and all kinds expect you to come up to their
different expectations. people scare me.

once i found a man in a filthy tenement who was a dying
alcoholic. he had at one time been a brilliant, suave, talented
personality who had made quite a mark in his church. one
afternoon, i took an older, much-trusted Christian man with
me, and after several hours of prayer in that tiny room, we saw a
wasted body and spirit touched by God.
and for awhile, literally changed.
it was awesome and beautiful.
i was caught up with a sense of mission and a miracle
God.
i so wanted this man to make it, to see God develop
"something beautiful" for his tomorrows. he began
telling me that this would only be possible if i became his wife and
helped him. i was totally caught up in the cause of his survival.

well, time revealed that i was off-course. my marrying him
would certainly not have been the secret to his survival. only God
was. i had some moments of poor judgment, i acted without
good sense, but God knew that never was i more genuine in
wanting a person to be His than i was then, and never was i any
more sincere in seeking God's direction.

i'm grateful that God cared for both of us.
we went our separate ways.
some people in my church will always tag me "a poor risk"
because of that incident where i almost did the wrong thing.
and i must confess i've been just as guilty in tagging others.
i hope i'm learning not to.

as a child, my parents talked often about the secret to life:
letting Jesus be Lord. today i have little assurance about
MY ability to cope successfully with all that shall face me in
life. i am more convinced than ever that if Jesus Christ controls
me totally, and i faithfully seek Him, He will move quietly and
constantly and protectively through
    the valleys
       agonies
           decisions
               incredibly stifling places.

as we experience life, truth will grow
in us if God is in us.

i will always, i guess, "see through a glass darkly" on some
things ... but i can't wait to ask God for just ten minutes of His
time so He can sit down with me and answer some questions i
have,
and clear the confusions.
someday i can.

today, He expects me to be a
woman—to fill the unknown, the uncertainties,
and the empty places with Himself.
to find the poise a living Lord can give.

prejudice

i grew up in hawaii.
   i was caucasian.
      but there was something
about the oriental-island culture
     that absorbed under my skin.
i found myself feeling japanese-hawaiian.
   or maybe i was wanting to feel that, because i wasn't.
   i was the minority.
   i went through school being one in a handful of "haoles"...
   or foreigners.

a minority isn't fun. you stick out.
   everything good and bad that you do
shows.
some natural instinct makes us want to be at home
   in and a part of our setting. an acceptable part.

my twin sister and i hung close.
    we cried a lot.
we wanted dark skin.
that was beautiful.

we were blue-eyed and very fair.
orientals are generally short and petite.
   we were tall and long-legged. most students
   were buddhists and hindus. we were Christian.
on our friends' coffee tables were shrines. on ours,
the Bible. it seemed in every way
   we were oddities
   in our setting.

the sun brought us as close to dark skin as we could get.
we spent hours on saturdays baking on waikiki shore lines,
   hoping to blend in with the others.
today, jan and i are still sun lovers. we still feel more
   secure with a tan. feelings one learns in childhood
are so hard to unlearn.

i find myself still working at keeping my back very straight.
as a child, i almost wished to be stooped rather
than peer over everyone.
                              anything to keep me from being too
noticed in what i thought was a negative way.

one kid who attended high school with my sister and me
was also caucasian, and Christian.
   he was struggling for acceptance, too. he struggled
so hard that he ignored us. i think i understand.
if he could remove himself from the minority
   he was a part of, then maybe the majority would naturally
scoop him in as one of them. it left us more alone,
more insecure about our personhood, more rejecting of it.

my sister recalls my mother or father coming to pick us up
   after school.
she'd always go stand close to a group of kids so my parents

wouldn't know she had no friends. we knew that the prejudice
existed.
our minority position stared hard at us. but we hoped
    others weren't so aware. there's some comfort in not being
pitied or openly rejected.

we feel prejudice about a lot of things,
but it's subtle.
                    that's the way most prejudice is.
we don't scream about it. it shows through in
    mean, undercutting ways.

there are lots of prejudices, and they always create pain
        and hurt.
often they are created for funny reasons, silly reasons.
they make church groups distant and cold and unable to relate
        as caring circles.

love heals prejudice
    because love accepts people where they are.
        how they look, how they act, what their potential is, or isn't.
        it makes no demands, no stipulations. it constantly
            reaches out and says, "you may be at one pole and i
                at another ... but can we be friends
                    and learn from each other?"

a close friend of mine is a journalist who claims to be
    agnostic. we met when she interviewed me for a newspaper
feature. she's pretty, vibrant, brilliant in her work.
she has a lovely family i'm fond of.
after we've been out together, and i start to leave,
i always say,
    "vera, i really love you..."
    and vera always responds, "i love you, too..."
    i laugh and hug her and think how wonderful it is that

even taking the most sacred thing in my life and seeing it as
pure skepticism in another doesn't have to build a wall. God's
    love streaks through the barriers. of course,
i wish vera believed in Jesus Christ. but we love each other
    in spite of our differences.
prejudice never lived in our relationship...
not even in the beginning.

when i was twelve, we took a tiny hawaiian baby to live with us.
she was a gift from her family who already had eleven.
    they considered it of highest honor to entrust us with their
twelfth. if ever a baby had love and attention
to grow in, lani did.
we were white, but somehow we were able to bring into our
    family circle the brown skin and black eyes that we so
loved.

God planned people,
    all of us.
under the skin or the type of dress or the difference
    of language or drawl...
under the facade of house and neighborhood and "what
does your father do?" ... similar hurts and feelings
exist.
        at different times, everybody cries and laughs
            and fails and feels embarrassed and insecure
                and needs warmth and someone to call a friend.
so when all the outside layers are peeled, prejudice gets
    tossed out, too.

love made me reach out again and again growing up.
not shoving, pushing love ... but love that says simply, with
    affirmation,
        "i am a person with purpose and value. i will be patient as
you work at remembering that..."

by the time i graduated from high school, i was no longer
   alienated.
it took time.
love does.
but the circle "drew us in."
   i felt belonging in the cafeteria,
      in the gym,
         at the bus stop.
love won.
it paid.

eric is my friend.
   maybe i love him extra because he's black.
i can imagine how it must feel
      in a white-dominated world.
he's six, and his favorite thing for me to do with him
   is rub his head.
      he stands tall with arms at his side, and squirms with
delight as i stroke his head
   and pat his face.
      "eric, i love you. it's fun being your friend..."

word came to me that eric was to go in
         for open heart surgery, and the odds were poor.
i was upset.
   i couldn't lose eric.
he had reason to live.
   the night before surgery, i drove into massachusetts general
hospital and went to the sixth floor; most of the children
   were asleep.
not eric.
clean pajamas, tucked under fresh sheets.
i picked him up,
            cradled him on my lap,
                        and rubbed his head.

"eric, you aren't scared, are you? don't be scared.
Jesus is going to sit right here by your bedside all night,
    just taking care of you, eric,
        i love you ... be brave for me."

i prayed with eric and tucked him back under, and walked
    out wondering if i'd ever see him again.
i did.
he came through.
he now scoots around on a shiny red tricycle.

i worry about eric. he lives in south boston.
    and racial prejudice is exploding and killing everywhere.
i hope my love for him makes a difference.
    i hope it teaches him that people belong together.
        all kinds.

in hawaii all the manger scenes at Christmas
    picture a dark-skinned Christ child.
        love sees no differences.

        Jesus, make my heart wide.
            so wide that differences don't matter.
            just beating hearts and minds.

legalism

a professor was lecturing to a class of law students.
   during his lecture a woman walked in
                                    and around the room
and then out.
the teacher continued talking without making reference to
the woman.
at the end of the class, he asked the students to write their
      impressions of that woman: how she looked
and walked and anything
they could remember. all sixteen students
      perceived her differently.

i have been raised
                  in the evangelical world. three of my
great uncles, my grandfather, my father, and two of my uncles
   are ministers.
i was fed and clothed and loved by the church.
   it is a tremendous heritage.
if there is one thing, though, that confuses and distorts
   my evangelical doctrine of love,
      it is legalism.

it is the law that dictates for everyone, anywhere,
    the absolutes of his/her relationship to
                                    Jesus Christ.

a student at a Christian college
        was about to graduate. extremely bright
and filled with potential, he fought one major crisis.
all his life, he had been raised in the church.
for years he had watched people "get saved."
he heard them testify the same way. they usually cried a lot,
        felt brand new and wonderful inside,
            and were going "to go with Jesus all the way."
i was eight when i accepted Jesus Christ
        at a billy graham film, and i confess
that is exactly how it happened with me.

david, however,
        had gone forward many times,
and never was able to cry
                    or have a high-peak emotional experience.
as a result, all these years
    he had decided
        he could not be a Christian.

one day
    he talked to a man who also was not an emotional personality.
he was reserved and rather withdrawn.
this man shared with david that Jesus Christ entered his life
in an undramatic way.
                    no tears.
                            no brand-new, cleaned-out
feeling.
            in his heart, he quietly and simply
chose to follow Jesus Christ. he confessed his sin,
    and began sharing his entire self with God.

that day, david's life changed.
    he had, for so long, wanted
to know God.
suddenly he realized that Jesus relates to our personalities
individually. today,
david is a strong, stable Christian.

one of the most beautiful stories in the Bible
    is about Jesus and the prostitute.
Jesus certainly did not approve of prostitution, but He saw
    that woman as a person
                                separate from her behavior.
He loved her.
He tenderly reached out to smooth her life.
    the pharisees' law for prostitution
    was to stone to death; no consideration of where the woman
came from, or what she
was in her heart...
just cruel, immediate death.
Jesus' law of love was
    compassion.
                "he who is without sin, throw the first stone."
with shame, i confess to throwing stones.
    i confess to the temptation of looking on a person's
        behavior, and letting that dictate my feelings for
that child of God ... of deciding for others what i think is right
or wrong for their lives when i have NEVER "walked in their
moccasins," felt their pain and hopelessness, come from their
    childhood. i acknowledge with gratitude
that more and more Jesus' command, "judge not, that ye be not
    judged," is being absorbed and understood in my life.

"perceptual distortion" is a psychological term
    that means we all understand situations differently, according
to our backgrounds and frames of reference. in hawaii, in my

strict Christian home, surrounded by ocean, for years
a major church function was having picnics on the beach,
    spending hours swimming and riding the waves. can you
imagine my shock when i moved to the midwest where there is
    no ocean, where some evangelicals feel mixed swimming is
        an abuse of the law of God? the difference
was in where we were raised.

        Jesus, after all You have said, over and over,
        about the pharisees and the law ... after all Your
        pleadings to be bound by love rather than law ...
        please help me and others, as Christians, to see
        people separate from their behavior that we don't
        understand or condone. be strong in us
        so we can always love people for being *people* ... and
        leave the judging to You.

thoughts

i ache.
the hurting i see in others...
wishing it were not
      there, yet ... knowing
         purposes exist
behind
every
cold
  windy
    valley.

i like that!
the simple
   unwavering
   assurance
that every task...
every dream...
      mission...
    winding road...
      every tomorrow...
belongs to us. You and me, God.

and lovingly and gently,
You will care for me.

i stepped up
by God.
it was as if
He really crawled
inside my soul.
for the first time,
Someone shared my secret heart.

i am not afraid
of my cross.
i would not choose
a polished, small one.

how i carry
my cross
will depend upon
the quality of my relationship
with Christ.
an extraordinary one
is my desire.
why compromise for mediocrity
when all of heaven and earth
were brought together
to make God personal to us?

i cannot achieve this
in a day or ten years.
or a lifetime.
but it is a pursuit that must
be continually active.
no matter how many times
i fail in my humanity.

evangelism

loving one another—
that's where evangelism begins.
how
can we change our world...
if we cannot even care about each other in our
    own circle?
pick a growing church in the New
    Testament.
how about thessalonica? everyone poured in,
not because the sunday school teacher was
    so fantastic,
or the curricula ... or even the program.
they didn't even bring in a special musical
    group.
but ... wow, how they loved one another!

there was john.
would our kids love him too?
shy. inhibited.
not too lovable. but they did love him!
not just on sunday, but every day.

because kids are everyday people.
they loved john every day until he smiled.
And then until one day he laughed.
his mother had called some time ago.
john in a flood of tears had said,
"oh, I'm such a failure ... but ann and the kids love me.
that's my only hope."
the non-Christian mother was impressed.
she started coming to church.

it's kids having the courage to tell each
        other...
"i love you"; "i need you";
"i believe in you";
or, "i've failed you. i'm sorry."
and proving it by day-to-day caring.
this is evangelism.

listen to our football players...
big, tough...
telling one of the simple, shy, ordinary girls:
"mary, i love you ... i really do."
no laughter, no silly stuff.
deadly serious ... really caring about each
        other.
"this is how to measure your love: that you lay
        down your life for your friends."
to pray for one another. to feel.

i came to a church with ninety teens.
ordinary setting. youth room.
all the regular stuff.
on-the-beat kids.
announcements.
little circle of weak singing.

regular lessons.
the works.
but i had a BIG GOD
who wanted to do BIG THINGS.
through committed teens!

So ... forget the ordinary hymn singing.
forget it...
the little circle of teens week after week after
        week.
the same old routine of drab commitment and
        blah faith.
expecting nothing.
and not much happening.
i refused to buy it.
not because i am some great expert.
i was totally inadequate.
but i did have a very special God.

if He could do anything,
why couldn't we start to change our world in
        exciting ways?
why couldn't we reach hundreds more?
i mean, if God is God...
Why little drab stuff?
so i began to pray: "Father, i'm Yours.
i have no real ideas.
nothing really sensational.
i mean, i don't even want it to be that way.
i want YOU to have total control...
i am listening. i am willing to learn.
how can we begin to change our world?"

and love came through.
more and more,

the concept of God's love became
        exciting to me.
God really loves me. He really does.
He laughs with me ... cries with me.
He pushes the hair out of my eyes.
He understands. He does!
and who can resist LOVE? who?

our teens began to prove trustworthy.
God could see that their love for each other
        was real.
nothing phony or fake.
it was the kind of love that demands hard work.
tenderness and careful understanding despite
        differences and disagreements.

more and more teens began coming to our church.
they loved sunday school.
they loved being loved.
they loved laughing and crying and sharing
        together.
they loved the meaningful love feasts that we
        had frequently.
breaking bread together.
openness, brokenness, oneness, honesty,
        gentleness.

an inspiration came!
CLUBS.
sunday school during the week...
for kids who couldn't fit into the youth room
        on sundays.
but...
for kids that needed to be reached. to be
        loved.

i began by picking teens who were strong,
        energetic Christians.
mostly from non-church homes
(Christ generally seems so much more exciting
        and alive to them).
would they like to start a club? could we use
        their homes?
would they bring their friends in from their
        neighborhoods?

so they started. the clubs.
in the cities surrounding our city.
freeway close.
it was up to the teens to bring their friends in.
to keep the clubs going. an action of love.

the clubs usually started with three or four
        teens
from the immediate neighborhood.
i loved the kids. i taught them to love each
        other.
i tried to help them believe a BIG GOD really
        loves them...
and that He is adventuresome and exciting...
        He can do ANYTHING
if we're committed to Him.
no pressure to build numbers.
just relaxed Bible study ... conversational prayer...
problems shared ... warm singing, joyful,
        gentle.
letting the Holy Spirit lead.
        unstructured.

friends were brought.
and they brought their friends.

and in a matter of weeks
we were running 25 ... then 40 ... and then 100.
and then we moved from the home to a nearby
        school.
wow! exciting!

in 1970 i had nine clubs a week. often,
400 teens, between tuesday and
        thursday,
being reached every week.
teens that would never have been reached
        otherwise.
teens that were
searching ... lost ... lonely ... confused...
        sad.

no way could we handle them all on sundays.
too crowded.
most of them without transportation.
no one to care enough to bring them in.
so we went to them
or they shared rides
to the senior hi breakfast club.
each wednesday at 6 a.m.
in the church fellowship hall.
eighty to a hundred of them every week.
catholics ... protestants ... jews—
from no church at all.
and you know what?
i wasn't satisfied with 400. i wanted more.
hundreds more ... lost and unreached teens.

nobody ... can really reject love.
and that's what we built around—
honest, growing love.

no emphasis on "don'ts" ... or even "do's."
we just tried to help them find a living Christ
who loves them.
we searched for
freedom, peace, hope, forgiveness.
to become strong and determined and committed.
beautiful!
through a living and loving Christ!

we were not too concerned about, "what can I do?"
but, "what can I be?"

we didn't have a calling program.
but we did have a caring program.
and individual responsibility is very important.
lovingly and gently, yet with conviction and
            force.
teens need to understand...
as do adult sponsors...
that "caring" is the most significant part of
            discipleship.
and i never asked our teens to be or to do...
ANYTHING
in which i had not first led the way.

i believe in a BIG GOD.
i don't decide to witness tomorrow morning.
instead i make hope and laughter and peace
            and poise and caring concern
a way of life with me...
because God is...

and it's happening!
a changed world where i live.

theology

"ann, you say 'Jesus is Lord' of your life.
what does it mean when you say that?"

He is my highest love.
not just on the feeling level—sometimes that can be a little hazy
—but intellectually, too. on the gut-commitment level.
   no matter how much i may love anyone or anything,
God's feelings and choices and wishes for me
   and for those i love must DICTATE.

how do i know what His will and choices are?
i don't, always ... in black and white.
at first, that scared me.
i have learned to think it is special that He gave me a mind
   to think and discern and sort things through.
He made me a person, and treats me like one.
Jesus Christ puts confidence in me.
He must enjoy the learning process.
                              mistakes must not scare Him.
He is not threatened by all we must go through
   to grow in His Name.

yesterday i sat at lunch with several professors.
   we started talking about our concepts of God. one mentioned
he had been doing some research
                              about God's wrath.
one looked at me.
"ann, you think everyone should just feel comfortable with
   God..."
he was a theologian. sometimes a mind like his
   scares me.
   it's too deep for me to try
to penetrate or lay simple thoughts before.

yes, i do believe God loves us to be comfortable
   in His presence...
      at home.
         unashamed.
            delighted.
when i have sinned or stumbled, He is the One i most want to
   be with.
first i want Him to know the grief and agony of heart
   i am feeling.
i remember as a child wanting school to be out so i could
      find my sister to tell her i was sorry we fought
         that morning over what to wear (as twins, we insisted
on dressing alike). sometimes
the path God chooses for me is almost overwhelming,
or i am not at all sure what truth is
   for me in a given situation. then, too, i want
to be very close to Him. it is safest there.
i am the most cared for and understood.
      only Christ can lift my guilt...
         can determine how honest my heart is.

it is when i have ignored God terribly ... when i refuse to accept
what i think He is wanting from me ... that i feel ill at ease.

God is God, and if i want to enjoy His divine Personhood
   in my life, and be at home with Him, He must be my deepest
reverence, respect, and loyalty.

wrath.
i think God does have wrath, but could it be kind of like
                                            justice?
i don't believe that weakens it.
justice stands
           immovable, for right,
and has no tolerance for wrong.
however long i live, i will believe
   though, that God, who is love, will always have mercy
   with His justice. He finds fault in us, but He does not
      tear down.
He seeks to bring love
               and to mend
                  and heal.

two:
on campus

dean of women

at twenty-five i became dean of women on a liberal arts campus.
some students were older than i,
    and at the most i was only eight years older than any of them.
vivacious, energetic, and stocked with what i thought were
good ideas, i blew in and took over.

it genuinely never crossed my mind that some people
would not be greatly enthusiastic about my coming (one can be
naive at twenty-five).

    older faculty and former deans of women must have
    considered me nearly a child, in knee socks and jumpers.
    others knew me only as a speaker, someone who could
    relate to crowds from a platform, but one-to-one?
    mixing into the emotion of life some solid logic?
    peers perceived my strong suggestions of how things
    could be changed as my wanting to take over.

i have survived four years.
amazingly. with gratitude.
through trial and error. feeling much growth.

some days thinking i am a problem-solving whiz.
some nights crawling into bed knowing no one loves me.

one afternoon i called a girl in to discuss the havoc she seemed
to be creating on her floor. i think i was relatively calm,
    non-attacking...
but before i could even open the conference with some facts,
she looked across my desk with blazing eyes...
        "ann, i don't like you.
        i don't hate you.
        i feel nothing for you.
        can i please go now?"
i wanted to punch every line she had given me with authoritative
accusations. my personal dignity screamed for defense. and
underneath everything, i was praying for wisdom. i realized
she was unable to deal with reason at that moment, and reason
was necessary.
i told her she could go. my prayers for her hence were
something like this:
        "God, bring beautiful things into sally's life.
        bless her. honor her. make her feel loved today.
        and significant as a person.
        create in her a sense of worth..."
i confess, on first impulse, i wanted to say,
        "God, sally's disgusting. shape her up, will You!
        she has so many problems, and she needs to know
        how disturbing she is. why should i take so much
        grief when i've done nothing?"

in those moments of inner conflict when i toyed with which
    attitude to take, love won.
God seemed to bring to mind that when a person is at
    tremendous odds with others,
    it usually indicates a lack of inner happiness,
    an insecurity about one's personhood.

54

as i privately prayed for blessing in sally's life, she changed.
warm smiles. friendly hellos. eased tensions on her dorm floor.
and ... i have to confess
i have laughed since and thought
she summed up my feelings rather accurately at times.
have you, too, ever sat through a very dull church service or
concert, and said to yourself,
"i don't like it. i don't hate it. i'm feeling nothing.
i'd just like to get out of here now..."
smile.
sigh.

parlor behavior is listed as "appropriate" or "inappropriate."
it's sticky to deal with. embarrassing, in fact.
no matter how many times i call couples in to inform them their
behavior is inappropriate and distasteful to others,
    they are always shocked and undeniably innocent.

often i understand the problem.
    some don't have any private place to do their kissing.
others have never had a romance, so the more they can display,
the more peers will be impressed with their flair. some like
to exploit their talents for further business.

i called a couple in for their parlor behavior.
after asking them to sit, i casually closed the door, sat at my
desk, and just as i opened my mouth to speak, a microphone
hooked to a cassette recorder was thrust in my face.
it startled me.
        "put that away."
        "no, i want to record everything you say so the whole
world can be witness..."
        "the whole world can know if you like, just by your
telling them. i shouldn't like to if i were you, but anyway, put
the recorder away."

(my human impulse was to blurt out ... "put that microphone
away or i'll shove it down your throat.")

how good of God to allow us to be human and not always piously
    angelic in our feelings.
how like Him, too, in those moments, to remind us how kind
    He's been in our silly notions. He has immense capacity
to see us where we are with gentle compassion and to balance His
justice with the right amount of mercy. it softens my reactions.

a girl cried at my desk.
her face flushed.
she wanted a certain room in a special dorm.
her heart was set on it. the curtains had already been chosen.
        "but, donna, it's senior-priority week. you are a
        sophomore. you must wait ... maybe for a year."
more tears spilled. her fist hit the desk.
"unfair ... how could i?"
i was ready to look up and say,
"it's been a lousy day for me, and i don't have to take this grief.
who do you think you are talking to?"
    suddenly, i saw me at nineteen years.
i remembered all the times my heart had been set on something...
the moments of frustration and disappointment.
        my voice mellowed.
        "donna, i know how hurt and angry you must feel. i have
        felt those things lots of times too. i am really sorry. it is
        against my integrity to change something i think is
        very fair, but i give you every right to feel upset. i
        understand. it's okay..."
she left in a flood of tears, and i went to a meeting. when i
returned to my desk, there was a folded note...
        "dear ann, you are one person around here who allows
        a kid to be human. i really do accept your position. i am
        sorry. i love you ... donna."

yes, as dean of women, i believe strongly in the necessity for
authority and control. i also know i am just as human as anyone
else...
just as vulnerable to hurt and insult.
so real that i, too, make mistakes and must say,
"i'm sorry ... will you forgive me?"

i feel, with e. stanley jones, that it is not so crucial how we
react, but how we *recover* in situations. when one girl plays
her trumpet at 11 p.m., and another reacts with fierce anger
because her rights to quiet hours are being abused, i really care
only about the end result: can they both listen and give and
take with each other, and recover a positive relationship?

anyone should be allowed the right to make mistakes. i would
not be where i am today if others had not accorded me that
right. i take direct and painful action only when the same
mistakes become habit, and the attitude toward growth, in the
Christian perspective, blasé.

when i must deal with a girl on a disciplinary measure, my first
question is, "why?" the answer does not demoralize my
decision. it just determines what direction the girl is going, and
helps me make a fair judgment that will not mar her future. i
know Jesus believes in that!

sometimes i must choose whether or not to be momentarily
popular, or to be more interested in trying to instill respect
and integrity into a girl's value system. sometimes i don't
know what the right answers are. i anguish through sleepless
nights, believing God is bigger than my confusion ... and more
interested in people than i. always i long for HIM.

i visit dorms late at night with a coat thrown over a flannel gown.
and a sack of cookies or candy under one arm. workshops

have been organized, and rap sessions in the parlor on
aspects of womanhood. i believe Jesus cares about things girls
feel. i have tried to bring Him to where they live. i have fixed chili
and fondue and cinnamon rolls and popcorn in my apartment,
and built roaring fires to sprawl in front of.
some nights i've lectured a parlorful of girls with enormous
curlers in their hair and mischief in their eyes...

> "don't whistle to guys outside your windows at
> midnight ... no more throwing water down the
> hall!"

they laugh, and i feel tired yet charmed by their youth ... but we
all know I mean what i say!

God knew i would love being dean of women on a college
campus. He understands my strengths as an individual, and
places me in settings where He can best utilize them at a
certain time. how special to know that God dreams because
each girl, through Him, has

> potential
> stretched and carved
> and carefully ordained
> for bright, happy, fulfilled tomorrows.

OH, JESUS, YOU MAKE MY LIFE EXCITING!

caring

i find ann so caught up in her own "tragedies" that
i often forget others have them too.

there was a student on campus whose wife was very ill. she often
couldn't sleep at night because of excruciating pain. when he
came into my office, he never mentioned the rough night
they might have had. he always wanted to know how *i* was
feeling. his words were usually,
> "ann, i just want you to know we have really been
> praying for you. your job is not easy."
they were actually able to rise above their own tragedy to
perceive my struggles. God had to have been in that love!

recently, a college graduate called me long distance.
"ann, i want you to know i am praying for you."
what did i say?
"bruce, i must be honest. i have not thought to pray for
you ... but, bruce, i promise today i will. will you forgive
me for not remembering to do so before?"
i hung up and thought of all the times i have told people i would
pray for them, and all the times i walked away and never did.

for the first time in my life i am wanting not to promise
prayers unless i really mean to pray.

it was a small room with just a few people. there were two
men. strong.
       suave.
             sophisticated.
                   informed.
i had never seen either of these men show emotion. i knew
one was really dying ... a personal crisis in his life was
destroying him. he was crumbling under it. suddenly i saw the
other of the two get up, walk across the room, wrap his arms
around the hurting friend, and hold him.
      and a man whom i had never seen show emotion
      kissed his friend on the face. the man with wounded spirit
      let one tear slide out and down the side of his face.
you may think that this is odd or funny ... two men
embracing, and one man kissing another. my father is very
feeling and expressive but i have never seen him kiss my brother.
in that room, however, on a night when the agony was too
deep for words to soothe, a rather emotionless man was
brave enough to "do" love through a gesture so gentle, so
powerful that it became an experience that has changed us all.
      one person really bleeding with another. not saying, "i
      believe in love" ... but feeling it, knowing what it is all
      about.

when people become a "body" in Christ, there is something
quiet and deep within the individual heart that nothing but
God Himself can create.
      then, when you cry, i really feel for you. when you laugh,
      so do i, because i understand your joy. when you say,
      "how are you?" i can look you in the eye and say, "i feel
      insecure and ugly today." i can say that, because when
      you asked, i knew you really cared.

i believe people can care about people. we can be at totally
opposite extremes, and still be friends ... still belong
together and laugh together. you may not like me as a speaker,
but you can see me as a person. no stereotypes or cubbyholes to
stuff me in, or i you.
   just people with hurts and dreams and despairs.
   belonging in His Name.

simple, strong hope ... "God gives a song"
for a little boy in chicago, cold.
an old man in a convalescent home who feels rejected.
for you who feel insecure or unlovely or unwanted or
   maladjusted or misplaced,
and me.
a song right where we need it,
a new song ... people unafraid to reach out and wrap their arms
around someone or take a hand or smooth a brow.
a song that makes us one.
   that gives us power to believe in a better world.
   that follows someone to their secret, silent hiding place
         where they weep and almost gag out their grief.
to them ... may the brave new song come through.

defeat

we just had student council elections at the college. today, i
noticed one of the students leaning against a desk. he had lost
in his race for yearbook editor. tender and sensitive, there
has been a difference in him. no sparkle. fake enthusiasm. i
thought i recognized a lot of hurt under the surface.

"how are you, mike?"

"uhh ... good!"

i looked at him quietly.

"no, you aren't *really* good."

his face reddened.

"you are a different 'mike.' no freshness. you're hurting,
    aren't you?"   .

his eyes filled. 'yes,' he nodded.

he came into my office and shut the door.

feelings began to spill. he was assured of winning. the loss was
such a shock. why would God allow him to lose when it meant
he would have to work all night, every night, to make
enough money to finish college? student council students get
scholarships. maybe, deep underneath, mike was wondering why
God would let his pride be so wounded, his self-image bruised.
did people like him? where were his friends?

it so reminded me of my sophomore year in high school. jan and i
hardly knew what football was until we came to mckinley high,
and had a team of our own to support. we became avid fans,
and lost our voices every single game, cheering. mckinley was
still "sellers" every year. smile.

song-leading tryouts came around. we were barely brave
enough to admit we wanted to run. we were so scared that it
took enormous courage to turn our names in and go every
afternoon to practice.

the ligaments in our legs were pulled. our muscles throbbed
with pain. my mother rubbed us with liniment, but when the day
came for us to go before an examining board for approval to
run, jan and i had to do just the arm motions. i laugh, now,
thinking of how funny we must have looked, and how earnest
we were. amazingly, we were approved. now we would go before
the entire student body and be voted on. could we pass the last
big hurdle?

maybe if children play in a lot of sports, they learn early the pain
and stress and disappointment that competition brings. in a
ball game or a swim meet, hardly anyone *always* wins. no
matter how good one is, there are usually bad days or frayed
enthusiasm or tougher judges or someone better ... sometimes.

jan and i didn't know anything about blood-and-sweat
competition. our self-concepts were poor. i think that's why
we so wanted to win. to be a songleader meant standing in front of
several thousand people and leading them in school songs in a
big stadium. it was the most serious thing we had ever done
to say in our world,

> "we are people and that is special. will you please say
> 'yes' to reassure us because we can then function as
> human beings who count in life."

to lose the race for songleader meant losing every single dream or hope we had ever had for being "somebody." meaningful life, itself, was on the line. i was sick with excitement, believing surely we would win. we were twins and that was special. they would want girls who "stood out." i was also sick with fear, that gnawing dull dread of the possibility of "failure."

somebody announced the results over the loudspeaker at the close of a certain day. several thousand students sat in classes, listening. the elected names were called alphabetically. when they passed over the "k's," i felt a sting inside i cannot ever forget. it was the smothering, gagging truth: jan and i had lost.

we found each other at the bus stop. our faces were stoic, sober, we looked unconcerned. inside, we wanted to die. it was a unique kind of hurt i have never felt before or since. it was so hard to face our parents with the truth, so hard to admit we weren't special (as we interpreted it) in our world as we had hoped. we went to our bedroom, and sobbed very hard and very quietly in our pillows. my parents were sensitive enough to accept a simple, reserved explanation from us. nothing more was ever said.

i didn't think for three or four years that i could discuss that defeat openly. today, talking to mike, all the memories returned. i understood. i treated his pride carefully, but opened his wound enough to let the hurt ooze, and ease the pressure.

an experience thirteen years ago became alive today so i could breathe warmth and compassion into a broken, struggling spirit.

my parents allowed me to be vulnerable to life's disappointments. they did not protect me from pain. for years they had built a solid foundation of a loving God in me, and then they dared

me to open wide my enthusiasm to be and to do and to give.
they cared for my bruises with dignity. i have always healed, in
time, and grown stronger.

many times since, i have known defeat: a speech tournament,
a queen's court, a job rejection, a romance. no defeat has been so
difficult as that first one. i am grateful for defeat. it is life. life is
where people live. people like mike.

self-image

a student dropped by my office.
"ann, i just want to tell you ... a lot of people don't like you, but i
sure do."
big deal! real comfort! so i have one for me and a whole lot
against me. phooey.
God must have a lot of faith in what i can become, because He's
so patient with me where i am now.

recently i had lunch with a friend in her kitchen.
a relaxed and warm place. wonderful food.
    she is always interested in me.
i shared with her my latest speaking and writing
experiences. it's always easier for me to share the things that
compliment rather than detract in my life, even though there are
sometimes equal amounts of both. sigh.

when i got home, i regretted not taking more of an interest in
HER world, not responding more attentively to her
twelve-year-old son. he is in a new school. just received an
aquarium. and had played in a basketball game the night
before.

that's big stuff. was my world too small to take it in?
no. i think my world was too insecure, my self-concept so poor
that i felt i had to help God in conveying that i was special.
special enough to be loved.

longitudinal studies show that children who look nicer, come
from better homes, are smarter, end up with more
recognition and love and attention. in the church world, it is
often the same. those with more money or social/political prestige
are more frequently recognized from the platform. people are
more eager to call on those with nice homes.
they look good. they smell good. they promise good
things for the image. they are needed.
the sad thing is not that they get too much care. it's just that so
many others don't get enough.

i have sat in groups where we talk with seeming great concern
about another's streak of poor behavior or shocking conduct.
we sound awfully well-adjusted and pious.
there are times in our work when we must consult with
someone re: a case. and then, there is always the need of
everyone to have somebody to talk out feelings.
if i'm honest, though, i'm sure that to spiritualize my
concern (to a third party) about another's flop is to try to
reflect strength in me. subconsciously or consciously, i'm hoping
it will distract anyone from seeing where i'm weak. as a result,
there are so many surface relationships with Christians.
God must feel sad.

i'll pretend others are the weak ones.
the troubled ones, the bad ones.
i'll pretend i'm one of the rare exceptions.
mature, "together," strong.

what a silly game. i watch people play it all the time. i find myself playing it too. i don't know why, when Jesus says we don't "earn" love...

He comes with outstretched hands, and strokes and smooths the rough edges in us, and isn't ashamed of where we are or our weaknesses and flops. He is ready to recognize us before the world. He has staked His life on what we can become.

HE IS THE SOURCE OF OUR INNER SECURITY, OUR COMING TO PEACE WITH OURSELVES.

criticism

love cares about people.
what they feel.
where they live.
how they hurt.

love is also open to criticism, and considers that there is
usually *some* truth in it.
love accepts the fact that mistakes and failures and
blunders are real, and love appreciates constructive, not
distorted, openness.

criticism facilitates growth. to think one is always right is to
be unrealistic. i have come home from a party, and had a
member of my family be honest enough to tell me i talked too
much. sometimes when i address a retreat or convention, it is
obvious i am not at my best. i sense people stammering,
trying not to be blunt, but finding it hard to say anything
positive about my speech. have you ever asked someone, as you
are ready to go out the door, how you look, and had them tell
you something you didn't want to hear?
i have. smile.

Jesus was honest but He always communicated His love. He acted like being human wasn't bad but should be talked about and worked with. the disciples seemed so secure with Him that even when He confronted them about jealousies or lack of faith or backing down in loyalty, they never seemed threatened.

He criticized james and john for their wanting Him to rain fire on the heads of those who wouldn't accept them (i've felt like praying that sometimes. you, too?) peter and others were rebuked for falling asleep while Jesus prayed in the garden of gethsemane. yet all of them became leaders of the early church. the fact they were corrected didn't mean Jesus lost faith in them. He simply wanted them to grow.

i wish Christians today knew how to love each other like that. so many relationships are shallow. most everyone is scared to unveil their real selves, scared of being criticized. we often end up trying to live in a way that will bring approval by everyone, rather than being real.

for me, personal growth and identity began to evolve five years ago when i was forced to face confrontations where i was criticized. previous to that, my immediate response was to find fault in the other person in order to draw attention away from me. only when i was able to listen to criticism about my youth program, some of my counseling advice, the way i dressed, how i tended to exaggerate experiences, and my need for reality in the euphoria did i find myself becoming a person that could honestly help people and be used by God.

a college girl once told me how hurt she felt because so many other girls on her floor said she kept a messy room. they criticized her for being sloppy. i smiled. i knew how she felt when she started telling me of all the ones she knew on her floor who weren't such prime examples of neatness.

>"gail, i've learned to listen to what people say about
>me. i used to feel so put down, and sometimes i still
>do. but i've discovered that there is often some truth
>for me. maturity says there is a lot of room for me to
>grow, and accepts it as a challenge. your mother
>always picked up after you, and i have a feeling you
>probably do tend to neglect your room."

we laughed together. she seemed to understand.

with criticism thrown at me that i honestly perceive to be
unfair, i toss it. forget it. that criticism does not matter. why
waste time stewing over it?

have you ever seen the cartoon of the boss who criticized
his employee? the employee then goes home and criticizes his
wife. the wife takes it out on johnny. johnny ends up kicking the
dog. all this because the employee refused to deal objectively
with the boss's criticism and learn from it.

for almost two years after i became dean of women, i was too shy
to go to the "fishbowl" where faculty visited and had coffee. i
was so afraid that they wouldn't like how i looked or what i
said. i feared they would think my ideas on life insignificant
and dull. as dean of women i was already such a target for attack.
when i realized all i was missing out on because of my fear of
criticism, i mustered the courage to slip into a corner chair
at the fishbowl table one day.

no, professors haven't always agreed with my ideas, or
approved of every decision made in my office. i have learned
to listen openly, even to laugh over some of my ignorant errors,
and i have realized that in a Christian community, we belong
together, helping each other with support and with honesty. we
need each other to be better people.

forgiveness 1

i remember sunday school teachers telling me as a child that the
most wonderful thing about Jesus Christ is that He "died on
the cross to forgive my sins." i really wanted to love Jesus
for that, and tried to, but i had such a hard time. basically, i
was shy, and always attempted to be good. i never could seem to
feel very guilty about "all my sins." it was not until my first
year out of college that i did something (do you mind if i
don't tell you what it was?) which engulfed me in guilt, that
terrible, awful feeling of genuine failure to God.
     for the first time, the cross lived.
     and the power of forgiveness.
     and the spirit of compassion.

recently someone i dearly love came to my office and began
honestly to tell me about the anger she felt toward me. feeling
terribly hurt and confused, i blurted out,
     "well, i don't like you either. i wish we had never been
     friends. i regret everything i've ever shared with you, and
     i haven't an ounce of trust in you."
she fled.
suddenly, i felt deep sorrow for my behavior. yes, at

twenty-nine, i actually said all that! i wanted desperately to be
forgiven. picking up the phone, i called her office.

> "i didn't mean all that i said. i wanted to hurt you
> because i felt so ineffective as a friend. i thought it
> would help if i made you feel the same way. will you
> please forgive me?"

as i have needed, over and over, to be forgiven, i have
understood how beautiful and necessary it is to forgive. not to
forgive destroys spirits and friendships. it becomes a bitterness
that poisons one's whole system.

my boss keeps a jar containing molasses and 500 pennies on a
shelf in his office to remind him of a boy who decided to pay a $5
campus parking fine in his own way. dean helfrich ordered him
in and chewed him out so severely that he was in tears.

> "i just did it as a joke because in my years here, i
> thought you were one administrator with a sense of
> humor..."

he ran out, crying. the dean of students came a few minutes
later, and sent all of us to find this student and bring him back.

> "floyd, i completely misunderstood you. i took it
> personally when you put all those pennies in that
> molasses. i do appreciate humor, and cannot go home
> to my family tonight, or do any more work today unless i
> know you will forgive me for such childish behavior."

the administrator cried.

> the student readily forgave.

> today,

whenever a discipline case is brought in to mr. helfrich's
office, he first looks at the jar of molasses and pennies just
to remind him how important forgiveness is.

love is diluted if there is a need of forgiveness between two
people. Jesus says we are recognized as Christians by our
love for each other. how sad He must feel when He sees

people sitting side by side in church pews and choir lofts and board meetings who have things deep inside they have never forgiven.

it was a church service. a man sang. he didn't have a good voice. it was weak and trembling, but he sang with such fervor and spirit that i wept.
afterwards i said to somebody,
> "that song was tremendous, wasn't it!"
my friend responded,
> "you know he was in trouble several years ago,
> don't you?"

Jesus Christ's redemptive care in the middle of that flop was probably what gave him something to sing about. i realized how easy it is for me, too, not to forgive people of their failures, and then see them as people with promise. in a home, there is more need of this than anywhere else. hurts are so unguarded there.

i know a woman who once was a vibrant Christian. a missionary friend, when home on furlough, would find this woman, many an early morning, kneeling by her bedside, praying for her. today this person is snarling, bitter, almost impossible to be around. somebody in her church said something about her that she felt was totally unfair. from a tiny seed of hurt, it grew into a poison that destroyed her zest for life, her relationship to God, her friendships. she refused to let God help her forgive.

i can understand how it happened to her. many times i have felt i've been dealt an unjust blow.
> but life has some injustices.
> and i've created some myself.
> Jesus knew how purifying and victorious forgiveness
> is.

"Father, forgive them..."

e. stanley jones says we are "Christians in the making." that means we should allow a lot of room for forgiveness.

besides, i have learned that Jesus smooths through and makes up for all the injustices in life ... if we give Him time.

freely ye have received, freely give ...

forgiveness
patience
compassion

forgiveness 2

people who have the most compassion and the greatest capacity
to forgive are generally those who are honest enough to
recognize their failures,
who are brave enough to have internalized their values
and plunged into seeking truth—not necessarily taught them by
others, but real for themselves as God unfolds it.

there are many i call my friends. we laugh a lot. we sip tea,
munch good food, and discuss our successes or politics or clothes
or others.
but there are very few of my friends i will turn to if i
fall flat on my face or get lost in the fog. there are hardly any i
totally trust. people who will never commercialize on me. people
who know how brash the world can be. people who will
believe in my basic good when the bad is showing.

most of my real friends are not church leaders. not ministers or
board members or administrators of the church. they live on
ordinary streets, behind plain doors, with down-to-earth
hearts. they are realistic about human nature. they have lived
and they have failed and they are honest about being fragile. they

can somehow grasp the enormous love of Christ. their hearts
are fertile soil for God to live in. they know that without
love, we are nothing ... and love is
>compassion, meekness, longsuffering,
>gentleness, patience, forgiveness.
>their response to life teaches me that God is LOVE.

if these people were removed from the church, and all the
hard-nosed, rigid, critical, pious, dogmatic Christians were
left, no one would come to God.
>at least, no one would come to God because they
>believed He loved them. they would come scared.

if ever there need be reason for heart, it is on a college
campus. students have broken away from their homes for the
first time. they are filled with unresolved bitterness, insecurity,
confusion, the need to know themselves and be comfortable
inside. the biggest decisions in life are suddenly staring at
them. they have to have some right to air their wings, and
fumble, and search. Growth usually happens through trial and
error.

dean of students bob helfrich is my boss. he is a real man. a
psychologist. a minister. a dad of two college-age children. he has
more integrity than any man i know. he is absolutely honest.
one always knows where she stands with him. he is human.
sometimes he gets defensive, sometimes he explodes...
>but the next day, it's all forgotten.
>sometimes, an hour later, a tear will slip down his face
>>when he asks you to forgive him for being so
>>human.

bob helfrich is a man totally loyal to his church, but not bound
by it; not playing games to climb to good graces. he is
committed to the institution, but his heart is always caught up

with the students ... where they are coming from and why they behave as they do. i believe i came to eastern nazarene college so i could meet him. so God could show me a committed Christian who forgives freely, listens intently, cares about people where they are, and makes no stipulations on his love for others.

when he was a child, he lost the father he adored. he listened to his mother pray in the night for some money to buy food so the children could eat. as an inexperienced kid, he was shipped to the korean war, and placed in the front lines. he started college without ever having finished high school. he's been through major surgeries, and heart attacks. one daughter was lost in a car accident.

> to learn to love must involve being vulnerable to
> life. to learn to forgive is being real. to feel compassion
> is first to know pain and hurt. it is getting down where
> most of the world lives and absorbing their wounds. it
> is the Holy Spirit alive and at work in our lives.

a senior in college came into my office yesterday. he has a tough shell. he tends to be loud and sometimes obnoxious. he likes to call me "kid" (which i don't particularly like), but he is comfortable with that so i try to accept it.

> "you know, ann, my mom died when i was nine. i was
> destroyed. i got so bitter i didn't care about anything.
> there were fights every day at school. the teachers
> would send me home. my dad would say, 'you go to
> school today and be good or i'll kill you.' when he left for
> work, i'd just go back to bed. i started hanging out in
> bars, and rolling drunks. nobody ever seemed to
> know what i was feeling. no one seemed to care. i was
> just rejected..."

he went to sunday school all the time. i wonder why no one had enough compassion to scoop him into their lives, to take time to find out what was making him act out so many negative feelings. i was glad for all the times i let him come into my office and cut up with his friends, even though often it irritated me and i wished they would be "more decent" in their attitudes toward life. somehow God helped me to accept him where he was, and in time, he was able to tell me where he had been. i see him becoming something.

he's going to be a teacher. i bet he has a whole lot more compassion and takes a whole lot more time with kids he'll find in the classroom because he knows what it is to hurt inside, and feel alone and lost.

three: people

magic of life

several months ago i had promised that tonight i would speak to
"pioneer girls" in a baptist church forty minutes away from
my home. this afternoon i felt irritable over the entire idea. i
was tired.

>girls in green beanies.
>all ages, probably squirming.
>so much effort in an already overstuffed schedule.

i bathed, donned a fresh long dress, and started out far from
enthusiastic. five minutes late, i blew through the side door of the
unfamiliar church just in time to be introduced. i hurried to the
platform, took the microphone, and suddenly broke into an
enormous smile.

>how does one resist dozens of girls with freckles
>and braids and ponytails and saddle-oxfords and
>beanies?

thirty or forty minutes afterward, i was still autographing all
kinds of scraps of paper which probably already are trampled in
the back seats of cars or blown to the wind.

                    i pressed my nose into some of theirs.
                        i laughed in their eyes.
                    i kissed freckles.
                                        i whispered dreams.

yes, i celebrated. it IS great to be alive!
some of those little girls are going to be lovers with me,
in Christ's Name, in our world. you watch!

in tennyson's *Ulysses,* he says,
                "how dull it is to pause, to make an end,
                to rust unburnish'd, not to shine in use!
                as though to breathe were life. life piled on life
                were all too little..."

even as a child, i believed there was far more to life than
"breathing."
a professor friend teaches maslow's self-actualization
theory ... the importance of BECOMING, of being AWARE.
he says that in a class of seventy students almost everyone admits
to never hearing a bird sing on the way to class, or actually
tasting and enjoying food.
                    i like cold water on my face, my teeth
                right after they've been brushed,
crawling between fresh sheets,
                                the sun in my face and wind
                on the back of my neck. it is great to walk
into a donut shop in the morning, and know the man behind the
                counter by first name, and hear him say,
                "i'm glad to see you, ann."
                flashing a smile at anyone, and watching the smile
spontaneously returned;
                            driving up my street, and the neighborhood
                children always grinning and waving wildly, and one little
boy always just screaming "ann" as loud as he can.

there is an enormous, droopy-eyed basset hound that
plops in the middle of the street, and i have to drive around him.
    he always makes me laugh because his life is so lazy and
uncomplicated.

one day i was racing through the student union building, on my way to
catch a plane. one of my girls ran up.
        "ann, where are you going?"
        "oh, i must fly to chicago tonight."
        "ann ... i'll miss you!"
for me, it is a tender, great feeling to know i'll be missed, even
when i'm gone only twelve hours. i threw my arms around that
girl, and hugged her tight.
        "oh, janice, i love you. it is so special that though logic
        is important, the real power in life is feeling magic be-
        tween people, i feel that magic with you. let's keep it!"

elizabeth barrett browning said it best:
        earth's crammed with heaven,
        and every common bush afire with God;
        but only he who sees takes off his shoes;
        the rest sit round it and pluck blackberries.

a dozen dark birds, wing-spread across the sky.
cold salt water crawling up the sand.
sky stretched with pink and yellow, and lazy limbs
    of old trees budding all over again, and again.
on early mornings i roll my car window down and
let life in, and laugh out loud.
                        "oh, Jesus, i AM ... and that's
        wonderful!"

to know my way around the city, to feel comfortable with my job,
to like my new sandals, to be asked to play tennis, to ride my
bike on a warm evening with a friend...

to have a cousin, a brother, a mother, a family ... to
say something innocently, and suddenly see it make
people laugh—and then i laugh because it is so
wonderful to see happy people...

to have someone reach out and touch me, or look
at me with dignity and respect, to have one person
like my sister that i can be totally free with...

to hear one bird on an early morning before i am even out of
bed, singing...

yes, yes, yes,

Jesus Christ streaks life with glory.

alleluia
alleluia
alleluia.

neighborhood

i always collect for muscular dystrophy in my neighborhood
because it is a great way to know my neighbors. this last year,
though, it was zero degrees out, windy, and i was two weeks
overdue collecting. i was angry at the whole idea of love. i
went home, put on a warmer coat, pulled a cap over my ears, and
started out. i whispered one prayer,
>"Jesus, i'm available."

i laughed with neighbors, and cuddled babies in hallways while
young mothers went to fetch a little money for my envelope.
finally i was down to the apartment next to mine, where my
newest neighbors lived. rose said,
>"ann, have you had lunch? come on in. i have wieners
>and tomatoes. norm is gone…"

we talked and visited, and rose said,
>"i read the article in the newspaper about you. you really
>are a Christian, aren't you? well, i grew up hating God. as
>a child, my parents constantly told me that if i wasn't
>good, God would punish me. and no matter how hard i
>tried, i never could do everything right. so i figure God

really is out to get me. and i think it's unfair that He should inflict so much fear into our lives!"

"oh rose, Jesus is love. He's not out to get you. He cares for you. He knows when you hurt, and then He hurts. He feels for your children, and knows the secrets of your heart, and never laughs or scoffs."

it was special. God had come to share with rose and me. suddenly i asked,
  "rose, would you like us to pray? i mean, i pray with my eyes open, and talk to God as if He were right here."
  "oh," she said, "i've never prayed ... so you do it, okay?"
  "Jesus, i love your putting us together as neighbors. thank you that we can be friends. today, help rose to know you care for the children in school, and her husband at work ... and help her to know you aren't out to hurt her ... that You are mercy and forgiveness and understanding."

i jumped up, hugged rose tightly ... "i love your living next door to me ... i must get back to school. let's eat wieners again!"

i walked out with laughter in my heart. you say, "did rose find Jesus that day?" i guess i didn't even ask her to invite Him in.

  she had hated Him for so many years, it seemed right that God should help me just to plant a small wedge of love in her heart...
  to grow and expand ... to give her time to absorb into her thoughts that He is LOVE and not unfeeling wrath. but some day, rose will find Him.
                              the wedge of love will grow.

love never gives up.
it is always at work.
 it pays.
    you'll see!

beauty shop

recently i was in the beauty shop having my hair trimmed.
it was crowded ... every sink and hair dryer filled,
women waiting.
the man cutting my hair looked up and said,
> "did you all know this girl is the dean of women up at
> the college?"
one lady lifted her hair dryer and said,
> "i don't believe it ... she's too young!"
> "oh, no, i have a giant of a God in me ... He and i do
> pretty well ..." i laughed.
another woman looked out from her hair dryer.
> "are you a Jesus freak?"
> "a Jesus freak? no, not exactly ... but Jesus is the
> Lord of my life. He is my Friend. He laughs and
> cries with me..."
and there, in the beauty shop, in an unexpected moment, on an
ordinary afternoon, we had a brief Jesus rap-session.

the next morning, sitting behind my desk at the college, the
phone rang.

"is this ann? you don't know me, but i was one of the ladies in the beauty shop yesterday. i'm a mother of four little girls. i am catholic ... but i never heard anyone talk about Jesus the way you did. could you tell me how to find Him? i want my children to know Him like that, too."

and from one suburb to another ... with a woman i didn't even know ... i shared that Jesus lives for everyone...

anytime...

anywhere...

and because He is love, He enjoys invading our lives. on a simple, uncomplicated day, i, an ordinary young woman,

touched my world.

anyone can.
right where we live.
Jesus can show us how.

gramps

grandfather was in the backyard, and it was mid-morning. his
small grandson kept begging him....

    "gramps, can i fix you a hamburger?"

    "no, honey, gramps is full. he just had breakfast."

    "hmmmmm. can i fix you a hot dog?"

    "i don't think a hot dog would mix well with the eggs inside.
the child tugged on his grandfather's arms, and burst into an
enormous smile.

    "i know, gramps ... a glass of water?"

grandfather looked into the dirt-smeared face. he wasn't
thirsty, but he could see the boy's desire to do something special
for the man he most admired.

    "yep, i think gramps could use a drink."

the child ran into the kitchen. he happened to pick up a dirty
glass from the sink instead of a clean one. he turned on the hot
water tap, instead of the cold. as he ran out the door with the
water, the mud from his hands smeared over the outside of
the glass, dribbled inside, and clouded the hot water.

    "here you are, gramps." (oh, his enthusiasm)

gramps looked at the awful glass of water, and caught the sparkle in the small face. he drank it all, and wrapped his arms around the lad.

"you know, that was the best glass of water gramps ever had."

sometimes my very best, however supported by
enthusiasm, turns out not to be so good after all. like
"gramps," God's love overlooks the muddiness and dirt, sees
down under to my heart.

with time, He teaches me the difference between a
good glass of water and a bad one, He smooths my
rough edges if i let Him ...

even when it hurts   terribly.   He mellows me.

the motto of my life is YES, LORD.
anytime. anywhere.
"yes" to whatever He wants, wherever He leads.
sometimes i have kind of died inside, saying "yes." it has meant,
"God, you can put anything in or take anything out of my
life ... anything You wish ... if you will help me."

you will seek me and you will find me
when you search for me with all your heart.

rejection

halloween was approaching. with tricks or treats. joanna was
three. her parents bought her a beautiful little costume for her
first adventure: collecting free candy. randy, her brother,
four years older, looked at her costume
          and boldly announced he was going to MAKE his,
               all by himself. paperbag and torn-up tee shirt
and painted face.

the night promising ghosts and goblins arrived.
dad took the two out. everywhere they went, people raved about
          how darling and special joanna looked, while quietly
               dropping some little piece of candy into
                    randy's sack.
nothing was said until they got home, and randy fell on the living
room floor, face down, and sobbed and sobbed.
               no one had noticed his "original" costume.

i am a twin. my identical sister and i were born five and a half
years after my brother, my parents' first child. he prayed for a
baby brother, and ended up with two sisters.

that was bad enough! on top of it, however,
was the fact that my parents pastored a rather large southern
church where a minister's family had not had a baby in years.
when the twins came, there was almost wild excitement. it
was 1945, long before multiple births were prevalent. fred,
who had been cradled and made over and adored,
                    suddenly was found standing, sober-eyed, while
church people flocked in to "care for the twins." how could
a five-and-a-half-year-old understand that suddenly he wasn't
as important to outsiders?

adult circles discuss rejection, and most frequently they can
point back to childhood experiences for its origin in their lives.
rejection is cruel and demeaning. it can be done unconsciously.
but sometimes on the conscious level, with some attack in
mind. self-concept and the courage to be creative and real
are usually bruised, and sometimes permanently damaged in
rejection. it inhibits and stings.
everyone is a victim at one time or many times.

though i am not married, couples have often shared with me some
of their problems. sometimes, partners reject each other for
inappropriate behavior rather than trying to respond to what
is happening in the other one's life to create such. one can
reject another simply by ignoring that there's been a hard day,
and the mate needs extra warmth and tenderness and
reassurance ... or by making the other one's ideas or needs
seem foolish and unimportant.

one particular friend of mine has several little boys. they are
healthy and handsome, but they have had some problems in
school. this is frightening to a concerned mother. another
woman, a friend, has a family also, but they seem always to do
everything right. they win all the awards, get top grades, are
recognized over and over for various achievements. Their

mother can do nothing but talk about how outstanding her children are.

she has a right to brag! everything she says about her "flock" is true ... but to incessantly share in front of the mother whose children aren't accelerating (in fact, they're struggling) is to reject, in a subtle sense, the woman who feels she cannot seem to succeed in her maternal calling.

there are people i call "friends" whom i reject in my own way. i know they are hurting deeply, because they have told me. they have probably told me because they needed support and someone to trust and they thought i might be willing to carry the burden of
            agony.
when i just by chance see them, i act like i care, but i never
            do anything
all the inbetween times, on my own,

                                    to show my concern.
i'm too busy. MY problems need time.
            no warm cookies. no free evening to invite them up to chat and let me listen. no notes. no time over tea. even in my office, they can talk while i address envelopes or answer phone calls.

        THIS MUST BE THE WORST REJECTION OF ALL:
                INDIFFERENCE!
opposites of rejection are reinforcement

                            and acceptance.

a man studying a school system was standing in a cafeteria with the principal. suddenly a little boy saw them and came up carrying a piece of paper. he went directly to the observer, whom he had never before seen, and wrapped his arms tightly around his legs and

hugged him. when he lifted the paper for the man to read,
his eyes were glistening.
                    "johnny has been a good boy today."
his whole self-concept had been transformed because he had been
            praised and rewarded for being "a good boy."
                    rejection was lost, a new spirit lives;
even a fresh beginning.

when i taught english, i had a jewish boy named neil in one of
my classes. he always sat in the back corner seat. he was
exceptionally small for his age, and the only boy in his family
with
            five older sisters. his father had always dreamed of
neil's being his football hero, and man-to-man partner
            in the family business. neil was very fragile and shy,
and sports was his farthest abstraction. he felt rejection
                    toward himself because he could not measure up
to his father's expectations.

every day, i would bend over neil's desk, look him in the eye, and
whisper,
            "you are very special. you have your own rare and
unique destiny. i am proud of you. you are becoming great in
your own way."

that was several years ago. i don't know what has happened
to neil, but i do remember that at the end of the year his
parents told me neil loved me more than any teacher he had ever
had, and he had worked harder and produced better than ever
before. i really was not a great teacher. my bulletin boards
didn't show much class. my daily preparation was less than
it should have been ... but i tried to totally accept and
appreciate neil *where he was,* and teach him not to reject
his own
            very sacred being.

jan, my sister, and i, grew up in hawaii and lived for hours
under the hot sun. at fourteen, we turned up with freckles
on our shoulders. we hated them. we felt shy. we felt terribly
rejected by what freckles said to us about beauty. when my sister
was about to be married, she mustered the courage to tell tom
that if because of the freckles on her back, he wanted
"out," he wouldn't have to marry her.

tom roared. he was stunned that jan should feel that way. why,
that was one of his favorite things about her. the freckles
were a girlish touch to her otherwise total sophistication. and
now, sometimes just for fun, he kisses them and reminds
            jan how much he loves them.
or he will blurt out in a dress shop when they are shopping,
            "i'd love this low-cut back on my wife, but she has
                  freckles and wouldn't want them to show."
and they will burst out laughing. tom's total acceptance of
            jan's freckles has suddenly made her not reject, but
            learn to appreciate, them. and me, with mine, too.

the saddest part about rejection in the Christian world is that
            Christians tend to reject the total person rather than
some unpleasant part of a person's behavior or style.
            as dean of women, i may not like a student's attitude, but
i hope i never reject the student. a girl may sin or make a
serious mistake, but God help me if i reject her because i
don't like her wrongdoing. rather, God give me the love and
insight to deeply love the person
                        under the unlovely or the
                              phony or
            the smelly or the obnoxious shell.
and in so doing, nurture warmth and trust and confidence
            to change and grow
                        and become.

the next time i start to put down
                              or withdraw
            or be indifferent toward someone,
i hope Christ, the compassionate Receiver, reminds me
            with painful awareness,
                              how much i have hurt
when i have felt rejection.

st. maries, idaho

i know a little mountain town in idaho where some
uncomplicated, beautiful people with dreams live.
          they are out to change the world of st. maries.
they will!

skip works at the plywood mill. there is one man he wants very
much to share Jesus Christ with. this man, however, comes
to work, crawls into the cab of his crane, runs the crane all
day, eats alone at noon in his car, and when the three p.m. whistle
blows, heads straight for home. he never speaks or
communicates in any way with the other men. a hard, lonely
personality, but skip sees him as a person Jesus loves. though
skip is not allowed to talk to him as he operates the crane, he
decided there must be some creative way to share. one day he
got the idea of writing two or three scriptures on his hard hat
about God's love and salvation. each day as skip hooks and
unhooks the tongs on the crane, this man must watch him very
closely to make sure everything is in order before he lifts the
logs.
          day after day after day he must read the scriptures on
          skip's hat. skip really believes he and God and the hard
          hat can change that man's life.

jodi has a women's weekly Bible study that has grown from a few to seventy-five women. she goes to her upstairs bedroom window daily, stretches her eyes across the town, and claims the women of st. maries for Jesus Christ.

bud is a three-year-old Christian. he is a carpenter in the mill. a sense of gentleness and wholeness flows from him to everyone. he believes he can change his world through paper. watch bud!

ben is in his sixties, and missing a hand, but that does not deter him. every week, he spends hours in neighbors' homes ... repairing walls, putting up paneling, roofing, plumbing, anything! he refuses money for his efforts. he asks only that he can talk about Jesus as he works. for years ben and his wife have hauled sunday school children back and forth to church. for years, muddy shoes have tracked up their car seats.

as jo ann drives twenty-five miles back and forth to work every day, her eyes are always scanning yards and sidewalks for children. she saw some children playing around a trailer house, so she got up the next morning earlier than usual and baked fresh cookies. on her way home from work that evening, she stopped at the trailer, and delivered the cookies to the mother. she shared her love for the children, and asked if she could do anything to help the young mother.

      jo ann, i love you!
      thank you for believing in dreams.

joyce works at the hospital, so that is her world. it isn't uncommon to find flowers she and her husband jim have had sent to the rooms of people they scarcely know, but feel are lonely and in need of care. she is often at the hospital in off-hours, talking to people about the love of Jesus.

george and taz work together in the woods. as they cut
down trees, they have made it a habit to sing and praise the
Lord. even above the roaring sound of chain saws, men say they
can hear them. at noontime, before they eat, they openly
thank God for His safety and the food. pete just happened to
work with them. there were many times when george and taz
helped pete and his wife out of problems. love alive in these two
men won pete to Jesus Christ.

> it's true.
> love always finds a way through.
> it shows.
> it heals the wounds.
> it wraps arms and hearts around hurts and confusion.
> love changes things!

a young pastor and wife, ron and marilyn, and their two babies
live in st. maries. ron loves the word "impossible," too. he
believes God is going to possess st. maries, idaho.

> just as inevitably as the snow melts from the mountain
> slopes, God's love and grace are being poured out in this
> community.

i've been to st. maries. i have listened to their dreams. they
will change their world.

> you watch.
> you wait.
> you'll see.

individuality

Bless God for making individuals...
>for feeling strongly that each person is unique.
>for taking that uniqueness and letting it be the force
>to crack through and beat out the rhythm in life.

God believed that a maverick spirit should live!

i had taken a friend in for dental surgery.
>afterward, they put her in a small recovery room and

permitted me to go in.

the assisting nurse was white-haired, plump, and pleasant.
>"it's all right, dear. one usually cries coming out of the
>anesthesia. that is healthy."

she cajoled and called out comforting thoughts in bostonian
accent, and fluffed the pillow and straightened the blanket and
soothed with a cool cloth across the forehead.

i sat there quite captivated by the skill and sense of mission she
put into her work. i went over and patted her arm, and waited
for her to look me in the eye.

"you are very special. you treat people with care,
            as if their feelings really matter to you. i'm glad
        you're in my world. i'm a Christian, and i think God
            must love and appreciate what you are!"

her eyes filled. she seemed so pleased. wrapping an arm
around me, she burst out,
        "oh, thank you ... thank you very much. no one's said
that to me before. i've worked here for fifteen years. i am
seventy-two. my husband has been bedridden for
twenty-four years. with bursitis in both my hips, i thought if i
could get out and help cheer others maybe my life would not seem
so overwhelming. today, your talking to me makes it all seem
so right."

she will probably never be selected for a magazine feature, but
she was born with greatness. the world is different...
        bright and warm ... for anyone who goes into that
            office each day.

a small boy was given a part in the Christmas play. he was
        to be the innkeeper that turned joseph and mary away.
        "i don't want to be that man. he is not nice!"
his lip quivered, and he pleaded for another part, but things were
rather rushed, and the innkeeper was the only character left,
and the director insisted he take *that* part.

the night of the performance came, and mary and joseph
knocked. this small boy, draped in costume, opened.
        "there is no room in the inn ... but if you like,
            you can rest awhile and have cookies and tea."
his young heart was not primed for unkindness. he said his line,
and then added another so he could be genuinely himself,
letting fresh love slip through.

most who are lauded for greatness have rooted it in individuality.
sometimes the rareness of personhood that makes a person
        stand out in a crowd
changes once the crowd rallies around. it suddenly seems
necessary and important to "click" with everyone, and then,
suddenly, the rarity gets lost and colorless in total uniformity.

i'm ann. really, if i am sophisticated, it is in a simple,
unmarked way. i would always rather eat around someone's
kitchen table than some "top of the tower" restaurant. riding
my ten-speed on a windy day and laughing because i am
breathless is far more fun for me than flying across country on
a jet. i like wearing knee socks and jumpers most every winter
morning. my hair is straight and short, and when i speak, i
don't know which things i will share until i crawl on the stool.
i do not quote a lot of scripture (though my Bible is heavily
underlined and worn), and i wouldn't exactly know how to
give a heavy discourse. my whole presentation is
uncomplicated and filled with very down-to-earth stories. i
find it easy to smile, and natural to feel wonder over a clear
morning sky, and i love to kiss children's faces and squeeze
them until they giggle.

yes, i have to fight sometimes to hang onto my personhood.
people want to glamorize me,
have me don ultra-sophisticated dress,
grow my hair long, or make it very curly,
tone down my enthusiasm for life and dreams and a great God,
criticize my not stating a "biblical" text each time i speak,
stop singing to people when my voice is so plain;
simmer my eagerness and freedom to tell people openly
        Jesus is my Friend and Lord of my life.

sometimes, in the middle of it all, i feel very insecure
and decide i had better conform more ... and then i scream,

"let me be ME!"
God willed me and planned my being.
He sees my uniqueness, dedicated to Him, as promising.
and yours!

one woman approached me after a service, crying.

> "ann, i am very shy. i don't talk easily with people, but i
> am very good at baking cookies. do you think i could
> show my love that way instead of speaking like
> you?"

my arms went around her.

> "oh, yes. i'm not too good at cooking. God needs your
> gift. children, especially, will understand."

a shy, at one time very introverted college girl hemmed and
altered all my clothes, for free. she was so skillful at that. she
would make girls' wedding dresses if they operated on
limited budgets. God must have so enjoyed watching!
He is now blessing her for being herself, and all kinds of doors
have opened for her to be with people, and she is becoming so
at ease socially.

my neighbors, the calhouns, live in a modest home, and shop for
every sale to make ends meet. every night, they have a hot meal
waiting for me and a cup of tea, and if my bathroom sink clogs,
dr. calhoun (a college professor on a Christian campus) comes
right over and fixes it. they have changed the color of every day
for me!

miss janes, who retired from a civil service job and now is
secretary to the dean of students, is skilled with typing and
shorthand. her real gift, though, is laughing hard at the
students' silly jokes and making each one feel his/her
problem terribly real and important.

sir winston churchill was once a small boy who talked with a lisp. growing up he was never a scholar. he did have a knack for english, and became one of the greatest writers of all time. when war came along, they rejected him because "we need MEN." he entered as a correspondent, and ended up with some medals. he once rose to address the house of commons, and they all walked out. he spoke to empty chairs and echoes. one day he became prime minister of great britain and led his country to a world war victory. he was born to lead and to inspire, and he carried a will that "never gave up." and he made a DIFFERENCE!

"Jesus, i like what i am because it was Your idea. help me to find adventure in my uniqueness, and not want to be what someone else is. God, if i lose sight of the fun of being me, then Your dreams of what i can be in the world will die. always help me to remember that this is Your way of being creative."

joyce

joyce was young, fresh, pretty ... and unknown to me. she
walked into my office in long beach, california, one afternoon,
introduced herself, and said she had heard of me from an
aunt in oklahoma who attended a convention i had addressed.
> "ann, my aunt says you believe in miracles. you speak
> often of having a 'giant God.' i've come because i need a
> miracle. and i don't know who else to turn to..."

she proceeded to tell me that her husband, a banker, had died
suddenly of a heart attack one day on the golf course.
> that their only child, a daughter, tracy, came home to
> discover her father was gone, and from then on didn't
> want to go to school.

she would cry and beg not to.
over and over she made her mother promise to be home when she
returned from school.

"now," joyce continued, "the doctors have discovered a
tumor on my shoulder ... malignant ... and there's no hope for
me unless a miracle happens. how can He take me away from
tracy, too?"

well.
i was young and inexperienced about God's ways. but as
director of youth at a nazarene church in long beach, i
had dared all of us to take God at His Word.
"if God is not a miracle God, how can we expect Him
to help us change the world where we live?"
  *you can pray about anything, and if you believe
  you can have it ... it is yours.*

i couldn't imagine a God of love taking a frightened child's
mother, when He had already allowed death to take the father.
i decided, on my own, that He would will for joyce to live.
our faith would be the catalyst in getting God's attention and
response.

the teens and i met joyce's parents, and tracy.
they sang for joyce with guitar and heart frequently.
we began to pray.
    each in our own separate ways and times.
      on ordinary week nights, we'd find each other around
      the church altar. joyce must live.
    gradually it seemed the adults picked up on it ... and
        everyone began fiercely to believe for a miracle.

one day as joyce and tracy were driving down san diego freeway,
tracy began to cry. (tracy was intelligent and pretty ... still a
child.)
      "mummy, i hear God. He's speaking to me. He's
saying you're going to live."
      "tracy, sometimes we think we hear God saying
things because we want Him to ... but it's not real."
      "no, mummy, it's real. i hear Him."

from that time on, tracy was no longer afraid.

the more we prayed ... the more strongly we believed ... the
worse joyce became. the tumor began to spread to other parts
of her body.

       but she laughed.
       she fought it.
       she had to conquer.
       God promised. "as our faith...'

eventually joyce went to the hospital. we were more determined
than ever. one day i took tracy in to see her mother, and tracy
prayed,

       "oh, Jesus, thank You. thank You because i'm not
       scared. mummy will live. You promised. help her not to
       be scared either..."
there lay Joyce, under oxygen, in intense pain.
and tracy was absolutely fearless!
many nights joyce's mother would call from the hospital...
       "she's slipping. please come. she's asking for you."
i'd throw a robe on, and race there. my faith, too, was
steadfast. without fear.

joyce died ... and i was called to break the news to her mother
and little tracy.

i drove through traffic, sobbing ... yelling out loud...
       "God, how could You! You promised! our faith was so
         strong but You didn't come through on Your Word."
i begged God for some way to explain to tracy so He wouldn't
forever die in her ... because at that moment, i didn't believe.

the neighbor brought tracy in. i scooped her in my arms...
       "oh, tracy, your mother's gone..."
and through shaking sobs, this lovely child cried,
       "she's not!" (with finality) "she's alive. God is
testing us."

and as i cradled her, the words just came.

> "tracy, your mom does live. she lives in the most
> perfect sense of the word. God did answer our
> prayers. she lives with your dad. she lives where she'll
> never hurt again. God is there..."

i took her to the beach that night to get away from people
pouring into the home, crowding a child's agony.
we ran hand in hand in the sand. our sandals came off. cold salt
water spilled over our feet and ankles. a spray would catch our
faces unexpectedly.

> the sky was dark, and a thousand stars lived. we sat
> with our toes burrowed in the damp cool earth. i looked
> over and saw the silent tears on tracy's face.

"ann, do you think there's a beach in heaven?"
"maybe..."
"well, i hope mom's with dad ... and they see me
down here."
and then her head fell into my lap, and her body shook.
"oh, ann, i miss my mommy..."

i coaxed her into having a hamburger and milkshake.
i watched her pained face through the funeral.
i was her "fill-in" mother at her school's Christmas program
one month later.
"ann, do you think my mom can look down and see me tonight?"
"yes, i think she can."

it's three and a half years since joyce died.
tracy lives with her grandparents.
she writes me often.
she says sometimes she has to go into the bathroom, still,
and lock the door, and cry it out...

she's in junior high now. she's strong and happy. her faith in God, amazingly, is less questioning than her grandparents'. in fact, it's not questioning at all. she's healing well. i feel sure tracy's a child with a rare tomorrow. she has heart, and tenderness. pain can soften you that way.

the teens and i ... and yes, the older adults, learned from that experience.

       that God always heals (but sometimes by death—)
       that God's ways are not ours.
       His ways are right, more strong and wise.
       time reveals that.
and maybe "acceptance with joy,"
       healing of attitudes,
          a sturdy spirit,
is the truest healing of all.

susan, a professional singer, was in a boston hospital two years ago, after a tumor was discovered between her lungs. her family had called from the midwest, and asked if i'd go in and see her. she was young and beautiful, and her husband, a musician, was very warm.

several months later, susan told me that after my first visit, she began to dream at night that she was a Christian too. she felt as happy inside as i seemed to be ... but when she'd awaken, she couldn't feel God.
He was gone.

       "ann, i was raised in a strong Christian home, but i've
       ignored God for years. i think He's going to punish me.
       i'll never be able to find Him."

       "susan, Jesus is love, love never deserts.
                        never gives up on.
         it is faithful to the end."

this time i didn't pray for susan's physical healing. i prayed she
would feel *loved*. i prayed it privately. after she asked Jesus
Christ into her life one evening as i sat by her bed, her
response through tears and a laugh was, "oh, ann, i feel so
loved...."

and she did to the end. love is a miracle, the greatest one of all.

it brought God to us.
it's eternal.

at times, people are physically healed.
i've been. it could never be a difficult task for God.
but it's not His highest gift.
Christ's tenderest extending of Himself to us
is His ability to take us as individuals,
        to know us through and through,
            and to choose, out of extraordinary love,
His highest gift, separately,
                        uniquely.
sometimes life. sometimes death. sometimes an added portion
of love.
but always what is best for us and those who love us.

yes, Lord ... the mysteries of life belong to You...

the pendulum swings

in everything beautiful there is a pinch of sadness...
somewhere.
sometime.
it seems to give balance.

i know what it is to love someone.
to laugh easily.
to bury my head and cry hard if i like, unashamed.
to talk plainly and bravely about gut-feelings.
to be unafraid of desertion.
but when those i love hurt, so do i.
their causes become my causes, in some form.
their disappointments and injustices are absorbed right in with
my own. i cannot be removed ... disconnected.

to bear a child must be a magnificent experience, born in love,
with health.
a child is born in pain, and with all
the wonder of soft skin and small toes and a brand-new world
and the first drink from a cup, comes
the falling out of swings and cutting fingers and healthy screams

saying, "i have the right to express!"
in the spread of growing-up years and birthday parties and warm
hugs in bed and red balloons and ferris wheels, there are the
moments when math isn't coming too well, or peer adjustments
arise or adolescence becomes overwhelming and the outcome
not pleasant.

one little boy i know has just moved into a new city.
he is shy and scared and at night he asks his mom to help him
dream of ways he can make friends.
"you know what, mom ... if i took snacks for everyone they
might like me..."
the next morning he walked out with popcorn balls and
cookies crammed under his arms ... and high hopes.
                              he came home that evening rather
                              sober.
he had found one who might be his buddy.
to have an eight-year-old, brown-eyed towhead would be so
special, but that would hurt.

children grow up. sometimes good.
                    sometimes for less than what is dreamed or
                         hoped for or expected.
the pendulum swings...
                    good to bad.
                    difficult to smooth.
                    comforting to fearful.
no one gets excluded from the "swing" in life. sometimes those
whom the world most glamorizes and adulates are those who
hurt and die like beggars behind polished, fancy fronts.

everything must balance.
if i want to love deeply, i should expect to suffer deeply. that
means i more or less choose, for myself, what i want to put in and
take out of life, nothing great or noble or deep comes cheaply.

no small, smooth, shiny cross.
a bigger, rougher, heavier one.

i have always had BIG dreams. i have always believed in an
extraordinarily great God. my dreams still live with no weak
streak in them, but...

        i never knew how much it can hurt to see BIG dreams
        happen. when one scrapes the entrancing veneer front off
        dreams, the reality of odds and guts and demands and
        costs becomes awesome. only
        a strong Christ in me can give me what it takes to
        become and do all He had in mind for me to
        swing with poise and steadiness with the pendulum
        of life.

        i think i'm up for high, wide-stretched swings.
        God helping me.
        that is adventure.
        you too?

four: en route

the difference

the day was fair, the wind fresh, and i boarded a flight going west
to speak at a conference. i had an aisle seat, close to the front,
on a tightly-packed plane.

a young couple breezed on at the last moment. the husband
looked distressed as he began to realize that the only two spots
left were middle seats on either side of the aisle. i bet i could
guess. they didn't travel together often. this was a special
thing. they wanted to be together. in the rush they were late, and
now ... they couldn't.

love for me is usually not something i say. it is what i do. my
mind worked fast. middle seats aren't my favorite thing, but if i
would move to one, then the couple could sit together where i
was. i gathered my things...

       "ohh, sir, you and your wife could sit here. i can move
       across the aisle to that seat in the middle."
       warm grin. "gee, you don't mind? that would be
       great!"
       (the two rather large women across the aisle didn't
       think so. you could tell. that would mean being crowded.)

i crawled over a lap, shoved my things under the seat, and tried
to relax. i noticed that the lady to my left had pulled out *i'm
ok. you're ok.* by dr. harris.

> "have you ever read that?"
> "no ... just starting."

and then she looked up and said,

> "you live in st. louis?"
> "no, i'm just going to speak."
> "what do YOU talk about?"

i looked her square in the eye, and grinned.

> "do you really want to know?"
> i think everyone should have the chance to back out if
> they want.
> "ya..."
> "that Jesus is my Friend. that He laughs and cries with
> me. that He knows all about lonely roads. that He's love,
> and love makes a difference."

well, she told me in certain tones that she was jewish—she
had told God if He'd bug out of her life, she'd like it ... and
ever since she had chosen that they should "bug apart."

> "do you mind if i ask you one thing? do you know
> what inner happiness is?"
> "that's the one thing i've always searched for and
> never been able to find..."

> "can i tell you how it happened to me?"

she nodded, and i proceeded gently, but with enthusiasm, to
tell her of the friendship and forgiveness of God in my life. she
listened. we visited casually. i asked no more questions nor
pressed for any decisions or responses. suddenly the lady on
my other side nudged me. surprised, i turned and noticed her
face was wet.

> "honey, i'm jewish, too, but do you see this?"

she pulled at a star of david on a thin chain around her neck.

"my husband was a strong believer in the jewish
faith. he was a heart surgeon, but died unexpectedly of
a heart attack two years ago. when i lost him, i lost
everything. i decided i wanted someone to tell me how
to find Jesus. Christians seemed to have hope. and a
man showed me, and i've been a believer ever since."

and with that, she reached around me and patted the other
woman's arm. "you listen to this girl. what she tells you is
true. i know. i am jewish like you, but Jesus has changed my
life."

the woman smiled and nodded.

the plane landed shortly after, and taxied in to the gate.
purse over my shoulder, and things under one arm, i stood and
started to move into the aisle to deplane. suddenly the man across
the aisle reached out his hand. automatically i reached out
mine and the grasp was strong: i thought he must be ready to
thank me for letting him sit next to his wife.

"young lady, my wife and i are Christians too. we've sat
across the aisle intrigued and thrilled by all you had to say.
God bless you."

suddenly, the woman to whom I'd talked burst into tears.
"...how come i happened to end up on a whole row of
Christians?"

one real, true magic moment! we all laughed.

where people are, needs are. hurts, searchings, hunger.
if Jesus is in me, He can reach out to them.
on a plane. at a bus stop. in a restaurant. at the shop or school.
He reaches out in things we do.

sir, my seat?
ma'am, take my hand.
did you need a dime?
can i help you with that?
tell me how you feel. i'll listen.
love makes the difference.

hap

i boarded a 747 one evening, heading to the west coast from
boston. it had been a long day, and the flight would be six
hours. i was hoping no one would be seated beside me so i
could collapse, rest, and not worry about conversation. but...
> a typical, sophisticated businessman had the window
> seat. sport coat thrown over his lap. wall street journal
> unfolded.

"hi ... i'm ann..."
"how are you? i'm hap."

and a little while later...
"do you live in california?"
"no," i replied, "i am just going to speak."
"you speak? what do YOU speak about?"
"you really want to know?" smile.
> "that Jesus is my Friend.
> that He is love ... and love is people caring
> for people. that because Jesus lives,
> the world can change..."

he coughed, and held up his hand for me to stop.

"i'm sorry. i think you've sat next to the wrong man.
i'm an atheist. i have five children, a Christian wife,
but i don't believe, and i'm just not interested."
wow. a real, true atheist. i hardly EVER sat next to someone
like that!
"sir, do you know why i believe in God?
i believe in God because He is love, and glasser
the psychologist says anyone in the world can make
something out of his/her life if there is just ONE
person to love them through and through ... secret
sins, flops, failures,
to share joys..."
and with no warning at all, hap turned his face to the window,
silently. i saw tears sliding down his face. nothing was said. i
hardly knew what to do because the plane wasn't even
airborne yet, and all i could pray was,
"Jesus, help him where he is really hurting inside."

i think people's feelings are sacred and private. i respected hap
for whatever it was that was happening in him. after the plane was
airborne for maybe ten minutes, he turned to me. his face was
red and wet.
"ann, i may be a dad of five children ... and have a
successful business, but i never have had anyone love
me the way you defined it a little while ago."
for six hours, from one coast to the other, hap and i listened to
each other. we shared. we cried. we laughed. we learned.
when the plane landed in california, and rolled in to the gate,
i gathered my things and stood. hap reached out his hand, and i
reached out mine.
"hap, i'm glad for you. and i believe for you.
remember, some day when Jesus comes into your
life ... in some quiet, unexpected moment, you will
know what love is ... and it will be wonderful. bye,
friend. God bless..."

124

two weeks later, i received an airmail letter from him.
it said something like this,
    "ann, those six hours were the greatest of my life.
      for the first time i really believed God is,
        because when you said, 'good-bye, FRIEND' ...
          i really felt i had found a friend. hap"

i am Jesus to the world around me.
you are.
His heart and hands and eyes and voice
and spirit of honesty and care.
you and God and i ... a team.
    we can love the world to joy, and meaningful and
      brand-new tomorrows.
      Jesus dreamed we would.

frances

it was a saturday morning. i had been out jogging, and had just
decided to clean the apartment because i was to fly to miami in
two hours to address a rally. suddenly it clicked with me
that i should check my airline ticket.

it was 12 noon then.
the ticket said my flight was 12:20 p.m.
thirty minutes away from the airport, unbathed, i knew i had
missed my flight. frantically, i called the airport ... four times, in
fact ... and kept wishing i could get a more creative ticket
agent on the line. but...

> he said i would have to catch a flight to atlanta, ga.,
> and go from there to miami. it would put me in miami an
> hour late for the rally, so i called the people in charge
> and begged them to keep singing ... i would be
> there!

i was disgruntled, but cleaned up hurriedly and caught the atlanta
flight. when we landed, i headed for the gate of my connecting
plane, and decided to stop in the ladies' room to freshen up.
dropping bag and purse, i washed my hands and put a brush

through my hair and started to leave. then i noticed a woman sitting in one corner.

"you have a long layover?" i smiled.

"eight o'clock tonight."

"eight o'clock! that's terrible..."

"well, my baby sister died and her funeral was today. this is the first flight i could get out."

"i'm sorry. i'm so sorry it's been such a hard day for you."

in my mind, i remembered someone telling me that the best way to help someone work through their grief is to talk about it. i put my bag and purse on the floor and settled in the chair (thirty minutes before my next flight)...

"my name is ann ... what's yours?"   "frances."

"tell me about your little sister."

frances began to cry, and tell me how she loved her youngest sister. what a special child she was. how unfair it seemed to her that God should take her.

"my little sister was a Christian. in a family of twelve children, she was the only one who ever went to church. it's so unfair."

"frances, i'm a Christian."

she didn't hear me. her thoughts tumbled into words and tears. it got close to the time of my departure, and i prayed for God to quiet her.

"oh, Jesus, how can i say anything to her? i can't get a word in ... please help me."

as she blew her nose and wiped tears, i started...

"frances, i know what it feels like to hurt. there's a little song i really want you to hear..."

"a song ... you mean you want to sing to me?"

"it's very short ... and you'll love it. i'll sing softly."

and i began to sing,

something beautiful, something good.
    all my confusion, He understood.
    all i had to offer Him was brokenness and strife—
        but He made something beautiful of my life.

"frances, even though your little sister is gone, Jesus is love ... and He can take this and make it a meaningful experience in your family. He CAN make something good and beautiful out of anything if we let Him. He can make something very special out of you..."

she looked up.
    "how do i find Him the way you have?"
it was so late. i took a paper from my purse, a scrap, and i wrote a prayer on it. not a special, memorized one. just a prayer.
    "Jesus, i hurt. i'm so lonely. i'm confused. Jesus, forgive me for being so far from you. Jesus, live with me. i need you."

she grabbed my hand. "ann, please pray it with me."
and i did, (silently adding a plea for God to keep the plane on the ground).
    "frances, i must catch my flight. remember, there are strong, happy tomorrows for you. Jesus is going to make this into something beautiful in your life."
    "ann, can i just tell you this? i'm a high school math teacher. no one likes me. everyone hates me. they call me all kinds of names, but their favorite is 'old battle-ax' and i deserve every name. but you are the very first person in my life to tell me i am special, that Jesus really cares for me. i was the middle child of twelve. i was homely. no one ever gave me much attention. ann, is it really true that Jesus can make something beautiful out of my life?"
    "oh, it is, frances ... it really is."

i ran to the gate ... it was cleared. the man behind the counter
was gathering tickets.

      "sir, the plane hasn't left yet, has it? i HAVE to be
      on."

      "lady, it is due to depart."

      "sir, there is a lady in the restroom who really
      needs something to drink. i know right where the
      concession stand is. could you just let me race out and
      get her something? it would take two minutes."

(in an aggravated voice) "well, HURRY."

i ordered frances the biggest paper cup of lemonade they have,
with a cap on it. i ran down the airport corridor and almost got
to the ladies' room, when i spotted frances standing out by
one of the windows, talking to a man. should i interrupt? would
she understand? i blurted out,

      "frances, you like lemonade?"

      "ann, i love it ... what are you doing..."

        "well, i thought you might get thirsty with such a
        long wait..."

people probably say, "ann, why?"
because so much of my life i have heard Christians who TALK
about love, but to me, love is something you DO. that's what i
learned in my home. a warm hand. a smile. a cold drink. a
meal. and i wanted frances to know my love went beyond
my words. i couldn't think of anything else but lemonade in an
airport.

suddenly this very rough, coarse-looking man standing next
to her leaned over.

      "is it really true what you've told frances? i mean, do you
      think Jesus could make something out of a rotten guy
      like me? i just got out of prison yesterday and am
      heading home."

"yes, sir ... He lives for EVERYONE."
when i boarded my plane in atlanta (i never saw such an angry
ticket agent when i returned to the gate ten minutes later ...
sigh), i cried.

> "Jesus, you really are love, aren't You! otherwise, i
> never could have found frances and this man. only
> You knew they were alive and hurting in this
> airport. Jesus, i'm so glad you are love. it makes all the
> difference."

john

i boarded a plane and was on my way to a speaking engagement. a little ten-year-old, tousled-headed boy was sitting next to the window and i had the aisle seat. we kind of began to talk. he wanted to know why i was going where i was going. i told him because i was going to speak. "wow," he said, "what do YOU talk about?"

i laughed and said, "do you really want to know?"
"yeah," he said.
i said, "what's your name?"
he said, "john."
"well, you see, john, i'm a Christian. Jesus Christ is the Lord of my life. He's really my friend. He really understands me when nobody else does. He really feels what i'm feeling. He laughs with me, he cries with me, he dreams with me. He makes something beautiful out of all my mistakes. i'm going to tell a lot of people that i really believe that God and i and love can build a new world."
"wow! that sounded pretty neat," john said. he'd never heard anything like that before.
"john, you go to church anywhere?"

"nope."

"john, would you like Jesus to be your Friend?"

he sure would. he never had a friend like that before.

"john, Jesus will be your Friend. He'll laugh with you when you laugh. and when you cry and you're all alone, He'll be there. and john, when you're walking down the street and you're pretty worried about something, He'll know just what you're worried about. and if you trust Him, He'll work through all your worries."

"well," he said, "how do i do it? show me how to pray it."

i said, "the prayer?"

"yeah."

i got out a piece of paper and a pen and i wrote a simple prayer. not memorized, not read out of some book. just a prayer i pray.

> "Jesus, i want you. Jesus, if You're love, that's what i
> need, because i get pretty lonely and sometimes i feel
> awfully unloved. Jesus, if You are the Savior then
> that must mean You forgive. i've done a lot of rotten
> things. would You forgive me? would You laugh with
> me? would You cry with me? would You really be my
> best friend?"

i handed it to john and i said, "john, tonight when you crawl into bed, will you read this prayer, and, if you really meant it, let Jesus come into your life? and be your Friend?"

"you betcha i will."

the plane landed.

i started grabbing all my things, and moved out into the aisle. suddenly i remembered john. i turned around—he was about four people behind me—and i called back, "do you remember our deal? remember our bargain? and the prayer you're going to pray?" he put up his fingers in a little circle like "i gotcha, ann."

132

i said, "see ya, friend. hey, john. that means you and i—we
walk together!"
he grinned, and i waved goodbye.

i wonder where john is today.
i wonder if he's out throwing snowballs, or cutting out
football heroes for his wall. i don't know.
i deboarded that plane already feeling the whole trip was worth it.
because i'd found a ten-year-old kid who'd never gone to
church. who had only heard the word God. who didn't know
that Jesus lived for him. that Jesus loved him and died for him.
somewhere today, john lives, and i really believe that Jesus lives
with him. and five years from now, or sixteen, who knows
what beautiful something God can make out of john as they
walk together?

Christmas eve

it was Christmas eve.
i boarded a flight from boston to san francisco.
i was going home for Christmas with my parents ... and it
     worked out just perfectly because i had to speak at
       a rally three days later, and that paid my travel expense.

magic was in the air.
gaiety and spirit and loud enthusiasm for life.
everyone was celebrating, and i just enjoyed
boarding a 747 to see what Christmas eve in the air
would be like.

in flight, a stewardess announced,
"anyone who is willing to lead the plane in a carol,
please ring your call button."
well ... if my sister had been with me ... or ANYONE else who
knew me, i would never have done such a thing because it would
have embarrassed them. i don't have a good voice, and...
     but no one was with me. i was alone.
     and it was Christmas eve, and Jesus was Lord of my life,
     and i loved Him, and it seemed special to do such a thing.

the stewardess led me to the middle of the plane, between everyone,
and handed me a microphone.
"is it all right if i sing 'oh, little town of bethlehem'?
that is my very favorite ... especially 'how silently, how silently
          the wondrous gift is given.' "
"you may sing anything you like."
i did feel quite nervous. so many faces.
when i finished, everyone applauded, not because i
sang well, but i think just because i sang.

a little later a stewardess came and sat across the aisle from me.
"do you love Christmas?"
"yes, i do. do you?"
"oh, i do!"
"why do you love Christmas?" i asked.
"well, i love watching children, and the smell of cinnamon
          and candles burning ... why do you?"
"do you really want to know?" and i smiled wide, letting her
          know she could back out if she liked.
"yes."
"because Jesus is my Friend. He lives with me. and when
Jesus was born, love lived ... and it has made such a
difference in my life."

the next twenty minutes were warm and genuine
and open and lovely.
Jesus on a 747 two thousand years later.
and we are still celebrating.

new year's eve again

God,
it's new year's eve
and i took a hot bath
and poured powder and lotion
and perfume recklessly,
and donned
my newest
long, dainty
nightgown.
i guess i was hoping
all that would erase
the agony
of being
alone
in such a gallant,
celebrating,
profound moment
when everyone so likes
to be with someone
to watch
a new year in.

it hasn't helped
too much.
i've tried to sleep
hoping that would beat
away the endless hours, but
after all afternoon and two hours
tonight, i'm worn out from sleep.
i've stumbled from one room
to the next,
wanting to cry...
scared by the aloneness...
more scared than ever before in my life...
but hurting too deeply to cry.
i've tossed an afghan over me
and casually
picked up a book
and tried to find intrigue
and inspiration and courage
from first a book ... and then the Bible.
but the words
crawled into my empty
heart and felt cold and misunderstood.
i did some letter-writing.
i didn't want to.
not when i often have to do thirty a day.
and i was thinking of something a little more
special and likeable ... but
i guess it did ease the pain some...
to scrape up all the words of hope one
can feel and find and give them to
another, always puts a little steel and bright-
ness into one's perspective ... but God,
i guess what really scares me is that
my family is all thousands of miles
away.

and
my dearest
friend is dying ... and i keep looking
at this past year and feeling disappointment.
there have been
too many weak moments
and fears
and hurts and
i know You're wearied
that i've spent so much time
fretting over things that ended up
never happening anyway...
i keep wondering
if i let You make of me
this year
all You wanted to...
and
if not,
does it spoil all
Your plans and hopes
and dreams for You and me
in the tomorrows?

o God,
the walls are so silent...
and there is no one around
to laugh and
change the subject...
i so wish for a friend's lap,
to bury my head
and let my tears spill
unabashedly and freely...
i feel tired
of pain and mountains and
grayer skies.

138

i so long for brighter, more
brilliant tomorrows ... yet i know
there is climbing to do
yet
to reach the peaks,
and i'm wondering, God,
can You help me keep pushing?

i'm not giving up, God...
i do keenly need more
grace and gutsy courage, though...

i just happened to think ... there's a
little grape juice left in the can
in the refrigerator ... i could
use the crumbs from last night's bake...
could just the two of us,
Lord,
have communion
at midnight?

five:
i love
the word
impossible

football game

when i was in southern california i received a call one morning
to speak on a large high school campus. the man said, "we're a
secular high school campus but we've heard quite a bit
about you and we were wondering if you could come to a
special assembly and speak to all of our athletes early some
morning."

"sir," i said, "i would love to. but i can't even catch a
baseball. what would i have to say to athletes? thank you very
much for asking me anyway." well, he thought it might kind of
give a boost to the athletic department. then, suddenly, i
thought of my motto, "yes, Lord." "yes, Lord," to
anything He asks of me anytime, anywhere. i said, "all right,
i'll do it. i don't know what i'll say but i'll be there."

and at 7:30 friday morning, through pouring rain, i drove to
oliver high school campus. i walked into an auditorium that
was packed—the football team, the track team, the basketball
team—they were all there. i walked down front. i picked up the
mike and couldn't think of anything to say except, "hi, i'm ann.
i'm a nobody. i'm lost in a big world. but i'm going to change
my world. you watch. you'll see, because i believe in the kind
of Christ that loves me." i shared my experience with them.

when i finished, two of the football members came up and said, "ann, that was just great. tomorrow night is our championship game. every year we play muir for the title. and every year muir wins because no team has been able to beat them. all the odds are against us. but, ann, do you think you could come and talk to the boys for a few minutes right before the game? it might inspire us so it won't be such a disaster."

by that time i was feeling very much at home with the athletes. i said, "yes, i would like to do that." but it so happened that there were several faculty members standing there and they said, "uh, hmmm, miss kiemel, that would be impossible. we're afraid you have forgotten that this is a secular high school campus and this morning was a very special assembly."

i love the word "impossible." it's one of my favorites because i have a giant of a God inside of me. i turned to the quarterback and said, "take me to the coach."

we headed toward the coach's office. i was just sitting there when in walked the biggest man i've ever seen— ex-professional football player, ex-professional wrestler.

"yeah, what do you want?"

"hi, sir, my name is ann and, well, i believe if you will honor God, He will honor you and i was wondering—well, you know tomorrow right before the game if i could talk to the..."

"absolutely not! i'm a very superstitious man. if we need a little help, we'll work a little harder on the field tomorrow."

everything he said was true. what business did i have marching into his office? all i could do was sit there and say, "yes, sir. i understand. yes, i know, sir." but on the inside i was talking to God. "You're a big God. You can do anything. if You want me on that football field, You'll get me out there." but on the outside it was, "yes, sir."

suddenly the coach turned to quinn, the quarterback, and said, "quinn, you won't believe this but, well, after talking to ann, i guess you can present it to the football team this afternoon, and if they want her, they can have her." but he said to me, "don't count on it."

i said, "thank you, sir, very much."

i could have walked out feeling this small, but i walked out with my head high and my back straight because i had a great Lord on my side.

that afternoon quinn called and said the team had voted unanimously to have me pray with them on the field minutes before the game. i was so excited until i got to the stadium and saw the thousands of people. the bleachers were packed. there were four extra rows of people standing and over the loudspeaker system the man said, "ladies and gentlemen, i have a special announcement to make tonight. we have the largest crowd in the history of this stadium here tonight—so many thousands of people." there i was, a nobody ann in her knee socks and clogs—scared.

the football team ran out and dropped to their knees in a huddle right in the middle of the field. the coach ushered me out and just gave me a shove right into the middle of the huddle. well, i'd never been in the middle of a football huddle before and i didn't know what to do. since everyone was kneeling, i assumed i'd better kneel too. so i dropped to my knees in the middle of that big huddle and i looked around into the faces of those big, rugged, huge football players.

i couldn't think of much of anything to say except, "hi, men. you're with ann, and i have a verse i'd like to share with you. you can pray about anything—*anything*—and if you believe you can have it, it's yours. i promise you tonight you're going to win. i know all the odds are against you. i know you've never been number one in the league. i know God sometimes permits us to lose to learn. but tonight you're going to win—but you're going to win on one condition—that you recognize that without God you are a failure, but with Him you can do anything. if you're running down the field tonight to catch a pass, or you're headed for the goal line, or you're headed for a tackle, i just want you to whisper one thing—'God, it's You and me.' '' one of the guys in the huddle raised his fist all of a sudden and yelled, "God, it's You and me." and another guy said, "yeah, God, it's the two of us." i prayed with them and one of the guys in the huddle said, "let's do it together one more time." and down on their knees in the middle of a huge stadium in front of thousands of people this football team that didn't know much about our Lord raised their fists in the air and yelled, "God, it's You and us." Then they slapped me on the back, knocked me over, and ran. i picked myself up and headed over to where they had a seat for me with the team. i walked with my head high and my back straight.

scared? are you kidding me? no way was i scared because, you see, faith to me is kind of like jumping out of an airplane 10,000 feet up. if God doesn't catch you, you splatter. but how do you know whether or not He is going to catch you unless you jump? i had jumped out and i wasn't scared.

in the first three minutes of the game one of our guys made a touchdown ... i mean the first three minutes. we were so excited. everyone was screaming and yelling and slapping him on the back. he pushed his way through and reached out and said, "ann, i just wanted to come over and tell you it was God and me." and he ran off. five minutes later another one of our guys made a 99-yard touchdown run. i don't know a lot about football; i do know that a 99-yard touchdown is pretty exciting. the place was going wild. they were crying and bouncing their hero on their shoulders. suddenly i saw him get down off the backs of the other football players. he came over to me, laid his hand on my shoulder, and said, "ann, i wanted you to know it was God and me. it was God and me all the way down the field."

to make a long story short, we won. number one in the league for the first time in history. i'm not sure if you've ever been pulled across a field by a football team or not, but they

pulled me. they loaded their hot, sweaty bodies onto the bus
and dragged me on with them. they began to scream and cheer
and yell. i said, "stop, stop, don't scream for me. don't yell for
me. i'm a nobody. yell for a big God who really came through
for you tonight." and with tears leaving muddy streaks
down their faces they began to scream and cheer and yell for a
big God.

suddenly someone said, "ann, can you step off the bus a
minute?" i looked around and it was the coach. i said,
"yes," and i got off the bus. he kind of pulled me over and
grabbed my hand in his two big rough hands. i looked up into that
rugged face and i saw the gleam of a tear in each eye. he looked
down at me and said, "ann, i've played some pretty great
games in professional football and i've coached some great
teams, but i've never watched boys play ball the way my boys
played ball tonight. i know it must have been your faith in a big
God. we are wondering if you could meet us on the field
every friday night."

i got into my little kharman ghia and headed down the
freeway laughing with God and singing at the top of
my lungs.

it was eleven o'clock at night and suddenly i discovered i
was out of gas. i had never run out of gas before in my whole
life. i was on the san diego freeway and i happened to be close to
an off-ramp, so i just careened off the ramp across a huge, busy
street and landed in a big, black dirt field. i had only a nickel
in my purse and discovered i had also left my checkbook at
home. there i was—eleven o'clock at night.

i crawled out of the car and said, "God, i know You'll send
somebody to rescue me." and suddenly i looked down. i
could hardly believe my eyes. there was a crisp one dollar bill
right by the front tire of my car. i got gas and put it in the car.
back on the freeway i laughed, but i cried through my laughter
and said, "Jesus, thank You for being great and for doing

big things; but thank You for being personal and for caring about me."

well, i wish all my experiences turned out like these. a couple of years after this football experience, i spoke on a college campus in the east. i told the football story, and it had quite a sensational effect. it so happened that the soccer team there was getting ready to play a tremendously competitive team, and they wondered if i would pray with *them* before *their* game. with a flair of enthusiasm, i knelt with the soccer team, on the field, right before the game, and with hundreds of supporting onlookers, we believed for a victory.

our team played hard and well, but they lost by one goal. now, that soccer team had as much faith in God to help them as did the california players, but they lost.

i flew home defeated and confused. it was not until many months later when i moved east to become dean of women, that coach jack, of the soccer team, told me this:

"i will never forget that game where you prayed for us, and our boys believed. we may have lost, but it was the strongest team in the eastern seaboard, and we played the best game as a soccer team in my history as a coach."

a former coach of notre dame always said, "the important thing about the game is *not* the game, but *winning* .... winning is all there is." i disagree. at the end of each day, i don't ask myself if i've been sensational in what i've done. i ask myself, "have i done my best?"

there are different ways to look at winning.

Jesus has taught me.

kaleidoscope

I'm a simple woman—young, believing—believing in our
impossible world because i'm linked to the extraordinary
Christ. i believe that He and i—through love—can do
anything. because love builds bridges, love crushes walls. love
breaks through barriers. love moves the world.

it had been a long day. i had worked hard at the college, but i
had gone to visit a child in a south boston hospital. as i
started to walk out of the ward, i noticed a young woman with
a tiny baby seated right across from me. i hadn't even been aware
that there was another adult there. i stopped and said, "excuse
me, i'm sorry. i didn't know you were sitting there. is that
your baby?"

she nodded her head. "a boy?" "yes." "what's his name?"
"dennis." "how old?" "seven weeks." a tear spilled out of
the corner of her eye. "we just learned today he's going to
live." "oh, how exciting," i said. "how tremendous, how
wonderful you must feel. i came to pray for eric—he goes into
surgery tomorrow. i just came to pray for him, but i was
wondering, would you like me to pray for your baby too?"
again she moved her head "yes." so i stopped and prayed for
dennis. i prayed that the world would not overwhelm him. i

prayed that God would make him grow up and to be a good man because the world needed good men. i prayed that God would make her a warm and mellow and strong mother, because only that kind of woman can make a great man. then as she wept, i kissed the baby, waved goodbye to eric, and hurried out of the ward. i was exhausted.

almost to the elevator, i noticed a tall, gray-haired, distinguished-looking man, standing at the incubator window. it was after visiting hours. i don't know why, but i stopped and said, "excuse me, sir, is one of the babies in that window yours?" he looked down at me and his eyes were red, and swollen. "yes," he said. "it's my daughter's. it's their first. but he's not expected to live through the night. that's my daughter over there in the white gown. they've let her in since the baby's dying."

i pressed my face against the window. "sir, this must be a very lonely night for you." i looked up out of the corner of my eye, and i saw a whole flood of tears spill out. "sir," i said, "i know what lonely nights are like. i've experienced a thousand lonely nights before, but, you see, i'm a Christian. Jesus has walked my roads with me. He's my best friend. well, i was wondering, did you need a friend to walk with you tonight?"

he looked down, his eyes swimming with tears. i just reached out my hand, and suddenly he reached out his and grabbed mine. he said, "i could sure use somebody." i said, "don't be scared. don't be afraid. you don't walk alone. God and i, we'll walk with you tonight, sir. there's a little song that i know would give you hope. the words go like this:

something beautiful, something good.
all my confusion He understood.
all i had to offer Him was brokenness and strife—
but He made something beautiful of my life.

sir, whatever happens tonight, he'll make something beautiful out of you and out of your family's lives. you watch, sir, and remember, you're not alone." i squeezed his hand, and the elevator door opened, and i walked in, and the door shut behind me.

sometime later i had an accident on my way home from work. my little orange porsche was totaled, and they pulled me out of the wreckage. two weeks later, still recovering from a concussion and bruises and sore spots and the realization that it was a miracle i had come out alive, i received a check from the insurance company with enough money to buy a new porsche. i decided which one i wanted, a silver porsche, and with another 914-6, and i was going to buy it from a young well-to-do jewish man named marty. he lived right down by the prudential building in the heart of boston.

my sister happened to be visiting me at the time, and we were driving into boston to pick the car up one night, when I turned to jan and said, "you know, maybe nobody in marty's whole life has ever told him that Jesus Christ could be his personal Savior and Friend. maybe nobody ever will unless i do. and jan, i've been thinking about it. i think i should share Jesus with marty tonight, when i pick up the car."

well, she didn't think that was a very good idea. i mean, it made her pretty nervous. marty was a sophisticated fellow and how was i to know that he wouldn't react very strongly to that kind of thing, and she said, "anyway, ann, i never know what you're going to do. you never tell me until we get almost there that you're going to share Christ with someone. and i never know when you're going to start singing a song in a restaurant or an airport." she didn't think it would go over, now, but i told her to be praying. just to pray.

it was dark when we pulled up to this big building. as we started to walk in, here came marty bounding out the front of the building with papers in his hand, and he said, "ann, really all you have to do is sign right here on this line and the car is yours. by the way, i have a friend who has just flown in from new york this morning." (i gathered that he was probably

jewish too. and i was kind of whispering, "listen, Jesus, that
makes me kind of nervous. i mean, trying to share Jesus Christ
with both of them. i don't know, Jesus, if this would go over at
all.") anyway, i knew it would be a little hard to try and
share Jesus with two men on a dark sidewalk with cars
whizzing by. i said, "marty, do you think we could go inside? i
have a couple of questions i'd like to ask you about my car."
and marty said, "well, sure, ann, yeah. i'll answer any
questions you have." so we went back inside to this small
office. i don't know much about cars but i dreamed up a couple of
questions. and he jumped up again and said, "well, i guess that
takes care of it."

i said, "marty, could you and jay sit down for just a few
minutes? i was wondering ... i really wanted to share
something with you. i feel a little awkward and frightened
about it."

"sure," marty said, "what's on your mind?"

"well, marty and jay, i know that your religious faith is the
most personal thing in the world. you choose to believe
what you want to believe. nobody makes you want to believe
anything. it's your own personal choice. and i know that you're
both jewish. for me, i'm a Christian. Jesus Christ is the Lord of
my life. He's my very best friend. He has forgiven me when
no one else could. He picks me up when no one else would. i
guess i just kinda wanted to tell you my story. how when i was a
little girl, my father tousled my hair and told me that it paid to
follow Jesus Christ. that He was love and He was truth."

i looked at jay and he was just wiping the tears, smearing
them off his cheeks. and marty was listening as intently as i'd
ever seen anyone listen. suddenly i stopped, and said, "marty,
what's one word to describe how you feel a lot of the time?"

"well..." his eyes began to flood with tears. he said, "oh,
ann, how could i put it in one word? i wish i had a whole lifetime,
there's so much i'd like to share with you. i can think of a
couple words that describe how i feel most of the time:

scared and lonely."

marty—sophisticated, handsome, well-to-do marty. scared? lonely? he said, "you know, i was raised in a home where it really mattered if you made money. i'm out in the big world, and now i'm scared. i'm always wondering if i'm going to make it or not. besides that, ann, i bet i'm the loneliest guy that ever lived."

and jay said, "could i say something?" and choking through his sobs, he said, "i just wanted to say, ann, i've been corrupted. the world has corrupted me. you're right. no one *ever* told me what you told me tonight. i never heard what you've just been saying to me: that Jesus Christ could really be *my* friend. i mean, i'm a jew. but He can really walk with me? He could really make meaning out of my life?"

"He could, jay."

"ah," he said, "that's what i want."

and i said, "you know, i have a little song i bet you gentlemen would like to hear." i looked at jan and she didn't look too happy. it was just as if she was saying, "ann, you're doing so well. now the last thing you need is to start singing these gentlemen a song. i mean, that will just blow it!" but i kind of giggled at her and said, "jan knows i don't have a very good voice. but i know if you heard my song, you'd like it.

come walk with me, through field and forest...

"marty, jay, Jesus does give a song. He makes something beautiful out of our lives. He understands our confusion. He takes our brokenness and strife and He promises to do something positive with our lives."

jay said, "well, ann, what are we waiting for? can't you pray for us?" and marty said, "yeah, i'd like to pray." by that time all four of us were crying, and we reached out and grabbed hands and in that small room, a couple stories above the busy, noisy street below, we prayed. and marty and jay opened their lives to Jesus Christ.

my sister and i got up to walk out, and jay walked over to me and reached out his hand, and i reached out mine, and grabbed his and he said, "ann, i just want to tell you something. you know why i flew in this morning? well, now i really know why. i flew in because i was to find you. i flew in because i decided after being in business, i wanted to go back to law school. i had a big interview here today. it was the lousiest interview i have ever given. the more i think about it, the sicker i get. for the first time in my life, i have a destiny. i never have before, but i never had Jesus before. so tonight, i feel great. i know if i don't get into law school, God has something better. and i know if i do, only God could have done it."

as we walked out of that building and down those steps, i thought, "destiny. that's what Jesus Christ gives." when we become a part of Jesus Christ, we stake our lives—our dreams, hopes, fears, our humanity—on the fact that we believe. we believe He lives. we believe He's truth. we believe He is love. we believe He brings destiny.

jan and i crawled into my new little silver porsche and rolled down the windows and breezed through the streets of downtown boston. i threw back my head, and began to sing lustily.

i was an ordinary person but i was a child of the King. i was linked to the eternal Christ. i had changed my world in a little way because Christ was love, and because He knew there were two scared, lonely men in the heart of that city, who needed to know what real love was—and needed to be linked to it. and someway, somehow, i had been able to show them how to find Him. the most tremendous thing in the world is for human beings to find that door, the door to God.

i love the word impossible. i'm not an extraordinary person. i'm a young woman with a simple heart. i live in a huge world where i walk down the street unnoticed. i board airplanes, lost in the crowds of passengers. but with God there are no impossibilities. give up? never. what is my dream? my aim? victory. because God and i—with love—with sturdy hearts, and determined daring faiths—will move the world.

you watch.
　　　you wait.
　　　　　you'll see.
　　　　　　　we can.